RE.

Equity in Your Coaching

sports coach UK is the brand name of The National Coaching Foundation and has been such since April 2001.

ISBN: 978-1-905540-80-8

First Edition
Developed from an original text by Annie Kerr in conjunction with Michelle-Vernon Way and Warwick Andrews

Second Edition
Revised by Simon Kirkland

The publishers would like to thank the following for their valuable input to this handbook: Andy Brittles (English Federation of Disability Sport), Liz Davidson (Women's Sport and Fitness Foundation), Heather Moir, Steve McQuaid (sports coach UK), Novlette Rennie (Sporting Equals), Sports Council for Northern Ireland, Sports Council for Wales, Sport England, sportscotland and UK Sport.

Third Edition
Updated September 2009 by Aj Sharma (Director of Crimson Tiger Limited)
Additional thanks go to Mahesh Patel (English Federation of Disability Sport)
Updated September 2011 by Sarah Cohen (sports coach UK) with additional thanks to: Nik Travedi (Sporting Equals), Lou Englefield (Pride Sports), Paul Whitten and Kevin O'Neill (Disability Sports NI), Justyn Price and Ceris Anderson (StreetGames), Annabel Kehoe (WSFF)

Cover photo courtesy of Alan Edwards.
All inner photos courtesy of Alan Edwards unless otherwise stated.

Published on behalf of sports coach UK by

sports coach UK
Chelsea Close
Off Amberley Road
Armley
Leeds LS12 4HP

Tel: 0113-274 4802
Fax: 0113-231 9606
Email: coaching@sportscoachuk.org
Website: www.sportscoachuk.org

Coachwise Ltd
Chelsea Close
Off Amberley Road
Armley
Leeds LS12 4HP

Tel: 0113-231 1310
Fax: 0113-231 9606
Email: enquiries@coachwise.ltd.uk
Website: www.coachwise.ltd.uk

Throughout this resource, the pronouns he, she, him, her and so on are interchangeable and intended to be inclusive of both males and females.

The definition of disability is wide and includes long-term limiting conditions such as mobility, sight and hearing impairments, as well as learning disabilities, mental health issues, cancer, diabetes, HIV/AIDS and multiple sclerosis.

The term parent includes carers, guardians and other next of kin categories.

To enquire about accessing alternative formats of this resource, contact the sports coach UK Head Office on 0113-274 4802 or email coaching@sportscoachuk.org

sports coach UK will ensure that it has professional and ethical values and that all its practices are inclusive and equitable.

Think back to the first time you participated in your sport. Imagine if your coach had said that you couldn't participate because you had a disability. What if your coach had insisted you wear specific sports clothing, but, for religious reasons, you couldn't and, therefore, wouldn't have been able to take part? Or if your team or coach insisted you change in another room because of your sexuality, or if your coach said girls are no good at sport. How would this have made you feel? It's unlikely you would have felt welcome and involved and, therefore, been able to progress to the stage you're at in your sport today.

Coaching is, first and foremost, about people – encouraging them to enjoy the positive benefits of sport and helping them to achieve their potential. Everyone should have access to sport, regardless of ability, ethnic group, gender, age, religion, belief, economic status, background or sexuality. Although we may like to think this is the case, in reality, it is not. Research has shown many groups of people are under-represented in all areas of sport, including coaching. For example, between the Moscow Olympic Games in 1980 and the Sydney Olympic Games in 2000, the proportion of female coaches in the British team fell from 9% to 7.6%, despite the rise in the number of female athletes competing.

However, at the Athens Olympic Games in 2004, although 39% of athletes were women, still only 10% of coaches were women. According to the *Sports Coaching in the UK* survey carried out by sports coach UK in 2004, still only 31% of coaches are female. This statistic falls to 18% when looking at qualified coaches. (In the *Sports Coaching in the UK Report* conducted in 2004 [MORI], coaches were also identified in the main as white, male and middle class. Visit the Research section of the sports coach UK Resource Bank for further information on this and *Sports Coaching in the UK II* [Townend and North, 2007].)

Everyone involved in sport has a responsibility to improve this situation – as a coach, you have an important role to play. Sports equity and being equitable mean ensuring your coaching sessions are fair, open and accessible to everyone who wants to take part. This means enhancing, applying and extending your existing skills and experience to meet the needs of present and potential participants. *Equity in Your Coaching* will help you do this.

The Equality Act brings together for the first time all the legal requirements on equality that the private, public and voluntary sectors need to follow. It affects equality law at work and in delivering all sorts of services and running clubs. It replaces all the existing equality law including:

- the Equal Pay Act 1970
- the Sex Discrimination Act 1975
- the Race Relations Act 1976
- the Disability Discrimination Act 1995.

Most of the new law is based on existing legislation that has been streamlined, but there are some important differences. One is the introduction of eight 'protected characteristics' (nine protected characteristics are referred to within employment law, the addition being around marriage and civil partnerships). The eight protected characteristics who use services are:

- disability
- sex (gender)
- gender reassignment
- pregnancy and maternity
- race
- religion or belief
- sexual orientation
- age (expected April 2012).

Although many different groups of people are disadvantaged in sport, this resource will focus on those groups who generally experience discrimination on a more regular basis, not only in sport, but in their daily lives:

- disabled people
- people from minority ethnic communities
- women and girls
- people from economically and/or socially disadvantaged backgrounds
- people of different ages
- people who follow different religions and beliefs, and those who do not follow any religion
- lesbian, gay, bisexual and transgender people.

The aim of this resource is to raise your awareness of equity issues and help you identify ways of becoming a more skilled and equitable coach. Technically, social or economic deprivation is not a protected characteristic and covered under the Equality Act, but sports coach UK feels that it is an important area to cover as it affects a large number of the UK population. By adopting the principles highlighted in this resource, you will help to make your sport enjoyable and accessible to all sections of society, and hopefully attract new participants to your coaching sessions.

Each section of the resource provides information, activities and questions to help you check your understanding and apply it to your own coaching. By the end of the resource, you should be able to:

- explain what sports equity, equal opportunities and equality mean and why they are important

- identify barriers that may prevent people from the key protected characteristics from participating in sport

- overcome the barriers that may prevent people from the protected characteristics from participating in sport

- be aware of the appropriate language and terminology to use when referring to people from the protected characteristics

- challenge inequitable behaviour during your coaching sessions

- interpret the legal framework that affects coaching and the implications for your practice

- develop an equity action plan in order to encourage involvement and participation by all groups and communities

- know who to contact for additional information relating to coaching people from the protected characteristics.

This resource supports a three-hour sports coach UK workshop that you are strongly recommended to attend. If your club is seeking Clubmark accreditation, the criteria require that at least one coach attends the sports coach UK 'Equity in Your Coaching' workshop. This resource will also help you put the theory behind equity into practice and apply it to your own coaching. All coaches are offered access to support and advice after the workshop. Workshop dates and locations are available from the sports coach UK Workshop Booking Centre (see page 108 for contact details).

1.0 What's In It For You?

The aim of this resource is to help you apply and enhance your existing skills and experience to make your coaching sessions accessible to all members of the community. Before exploring exactly how to do this, it is important you understand the concepts of sports equity, equal opportunities and equality, and why they are so important. The terms are used in general language, but are not often defined and explained in sporting and coaching contexts. However, this section will provide you with useful background information and help you to understand that equality in sport is about improving sporting opportunities for everyone, while making sure everyone is treated fairly.

By the end of the section, you should be able to explain:

- what sports equity, equal opportunities and equality mean, and the differences between them

- which groups of people are regularly disadvantaged in sport

- why sports equity is important.

1.1 What do Sports Equity, Equal Opportunities and Equality Mean?

> Sports equity is about fairness in sport, equality of access, recognising inequalities and taking steps to address them. It is about changing the culture and structure of sport to ensure that it becomes equally accessible to everyone in society.
>
> Sport England, 2000[1]

Achieving sports equity depends on everybody involved in sport:

- recognising that certain groups of people are disadvantaged[2] and may, therefore, be discriminated[3]

against because of their gender, age, race, disability, social or economic background, religion, belief or sexual orientation, not just in sport, but in society in general

- treating everyone equally, but recognising that some groups of people have different needs

- recognising the need to change attitudes, systems and processes to better meet the needs of all groups and communities

- sharing resources and making sport accessible to all.

Equal Opportunities

Equal opportunities is about the law and how it is applied in the workplace. The law only intervenes when it is clear that legislation is the only way to deal with discriminative acts (ie where people are treated less favourably in the provision of goods, services and facilities, as well as in employment). Therefore, equal opportunities is about ensuring employment practices are fair and that the workplace is an environment free from discrimination and harassment. Employers are required to comply with UK and EU discrimination legislation.

Equality

Equality is the state of being equal – treating individuals equally, which does not necessarily mean treating people the same. In some cases, the need for equality may require unequal effort, to ensure the principle of equality is achieved.

1.2 Who is Disadvantaged in Sport?

Everyone is treated unfairly in some way at times – no doubt you can think of a few occasions when you've been on the receiving end of unfair treatment. The following activity asks you to think of an example based on your own experiences.

---

[1] Sport England (2000) *Making English Sport Inclusive: Equity Guidelines for Governing Bodies*. London: Sport England. Ref no: SE/1043/1M/6/00

[2] and [3] For definitions of terms associated with sports equity, see Appendix A (page 109).

ACTIVITY 1

Think of an incident, not necessarily in sport, when you felt you were treated unfairly. Make a brief note of the incident in the space provided below and answer the questions that follow.

....

....

....

....

Why do you think you were treated unfairly?

....

....

....

....

....

How did this make you feel?

....

....

....

....

....

What effect did it have on you?

....

....

....

....

....

What did you do about it?

....

....

....

....

....

....

Now, compare your experience as a coach with those described in the following scenarios:

Scenario 1

David is a wheelchair user and a coach at a local table tennis club. The club has had a very successful season and is in a good position to win the league, with David being an important member of the coaching team. The head coach wants to move the training sessions to what he feels is a better venue, nearer to where he lives. However, this venue is not accessible to wheelchairs – there are no parking facilities, no ramp up to the main entrance, only steps, and the changing rooms are very small and cramped.

Scenario 2

Palvinda is Asian and has been a member of her local netball club for some time. She has recently been selected for the club team and will be competing regularly in local and regional tournaments. Her coach insists that all team members wear the official team kit during training sessions and at all competitions. However, this includes a sports skirt, which Palvinda cannot wear due to her close adherence to her religion – she usually wears tracksuit bottoms instead.

Scenario 3

Jackie is an avid squash player and has been top of the women's squash ladder at her local club for several months. To make things more challenging and improve her game further, she asks if she can join the men's squash ladder instead. However, the club chairperson says this is against club regulations and that the men wouldn't think she was good enough to play.

Scenario 4

Tracey has been a youth coach for 20 years and has coached a number of successful teams, as well as developing a number of players who have continued playing after they have left her teams. Tracey has applied for the position of county youth coach, which is a paid position. She later discovers the position has been given to a coach who has the same qualifications, but who is 15 years younger and lacks the experience she possesses.

Scenario 5

Kerry always turns up late to training sessions. The coach drops her from the squad after she is late for the third consecutive session. She lives in an area of high deprivation and is unable to get a lift by car or afford a taxi to the coaching session, like other participants. She has to wait for a bus, so she is unable to get to the coaching session on time.

Scenario 6

Steve plays for his hockey team and mentioned to the captain that he is going to the club Christmas party with his partner, Peter. The captain informs Steve that the party is for female partners only, and following this, Steve is asked to change at home before coming to training or matches.

David, Palvinda, Jackie, Tracey, Kerry and Steve all have something in common – they all feel they have been treated unfairly in their sport, What do you think?

- David feels that, by suggesting the club venue is moved, the head coach is acting unfairly. Although probably not intending to discriminate against David, he has failed to realise how difficult it will make things for him. It'll be harder for David to get to the venue and, once he's there, it will be difficult for him to get into the building itself, as well as make use of the changing facilities.

- Palvinda feels her coach is acting insensitively, insisting she wears a sports skirt, particularly as wearing tracksuit bottoms instead would pose no threat to her safety. Perhaps a compromise is for Palvinda to wear her sports skirt over her tracksuit bottoms.

- Jackie feels she is being treated unfairly because she is a woman. She is annoyed the club chairperson assumes the men will think she's not good enough to play against them and that he refuses to consider reviewing club regulations or giving her the opportunity to prove her ability.

- Tracey feels she has been treated unfairly because of her age. She is disappointed the county committee felt a younger person with less experience could do the job better, as this is a position Tracey has been aiming for, to further improve her coaching and seek the opportunity to move on to the next level of coach education.

- Kerry feels she is being treated unfairly as she does not have the ability of other participants to get to sessions on time, as her family cannot afford a car or a taxi to get her to the session. She is disappointed and frustrated as she always works very hard in training sessions, and always competes well in competitions. There is clearly a balance required in this situation. Attending the sessions on time is important, and Kerry, the coach and fellow players should make every effort to gain or provide the necessary support.

- Steve feels very unfairly treated because of his sexuality, as he cannot bring his long-standing partner to the Christmas party and has to change in another changing room or at home before playing the sport he loves.

Although many different groups of people are disadvantaged in sport, David, Palvinda, Jackie, Tracey, Kerry and Steve each belong to particular groups of people who generally experience discrimination on a more regular basis, not only in sport, but in their daily lives.

Points of Interest

- Disabled people

- People from minority ethnic communities

- Women and girls

- Economically disadvantaged people

- People of different ages

- People who follow different religions or beliefs, or indeed no religion

- Gay, lesbian, bisexual and transgender people.

This resource will focus on these groups. The term 'protected characteristics' will be used when referring to these groups of people collectively.

Remember!

- For ease of reference, the guidance in this resource is often divided into separate sections for each of the protected characteristics. However, this doesn't mean each group should be treated in isolation. Remember, some of the people you coach may belong to a combination of groups (eg Asian women, disabled participants from minority ethnic communities), so it's important to understand the needs of all the protected characteristics.

- Although this resource concentrates on these protected characteristics, remember these aren't the only ones, and other groups of people may be disadvantaged in your sport. It's important to identify who these people are and to seek specific advice from appropriate sources.

- In addition, it is important to note there are many differences within each of the protected characteristics. All Asian people are not the same – the needs of Indians, Pakistanis, Sri Lankans and Bangladeshis will be different. The same applies to all the different impairments under the general banner of disability, such as visual impairment, hearing impairment, people with cerebral palsy or, indeed, learning disabilities.

1.3 Why is Sports Equity Important?

Think back to the main elements of the sports equity definition introduced on page 1, where it was identified that inequalities need to be identified before action can be taken.

Recognising Inequalities

National Population
A primary aim of addressing inequalities is to work towards ensuring participants in sport are reflective of society. For example, the 2001 Census revealed the population for England and Wales included:

- 51.4% women

- approximately 17% disabled people (depending upon the classification)

- 10% of people from minority ethnic communities.

Sports Participation in the UK

However, a survey[4] carried out by the Office of National Statistics, on behalf of Sport England, revealed the overall participation rate for:

- minority ethnic communities is 40%, compared with a national average of 46%

- men from minority ethnic communities is 49%, compared with a national average of 54%

- women from minority ethnic communities is 32%, compared with a national average of 39%.

The findings of the survey also concluded the picture is much more complex than simply looking at participation rates suggests, as there is considerable variation in the levels of participation between:

- men and women

- different ethnic groups

- different sports.

For example, on average, the participation rates for Black Caribbean (39%), Indian (39%) and, in particular, Pakistani (31%) and Bangladeshi (30%) populations are below the national average (46%). Only the participation rate for the Black Other group (60%) is higher than the national average.

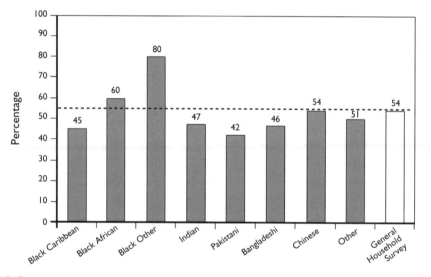

Figure 1: Participation in at least one activity (excluding walking) over the last four weeks (all men)

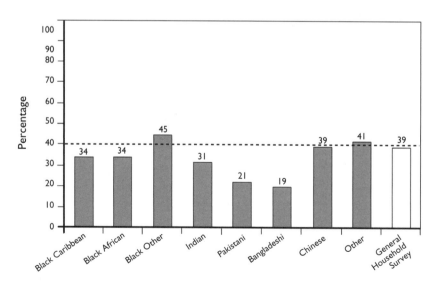

Adapted from the Office of National Statistics Survey

Figure 2: Participation in at least one activity (excluding walking) over the last four weeks (all women)

[4] Rowe, N. and Champion, R. (2000) *Sports Participation and Ethnicity in England: National Survey 1999/2000 Headline Findings*. London: Sport England. Ref no: SE/1073

The survey also recognised that, in some sports, participation rates for people from minority ethnic communities are relatively high.

In 2002, Sport England integrated the results of the General Household Survey and the Young People's Sports Survey for England, and produced the Sports Equity Index. The Sports Equity Index has been formulated to provide the evidence base for sports equity policy and initiatives in England, and attempts to estimate the relative propensity of different groups within the protected characteristics to participate in sport. It was devised to:

- assist all those involved in sports development to better understand the levels of inequality that currently exist in sports participation

- provide the evidence base for determining policy priorities, setting targets, allocating resources and measuring achievements.

In Scotland, surveys of attitudes found some interesting perceptions about sport. In all but the youngest age groups, people from minority ethnic communities participate in sport and physical education less frequently than indigenous white people of the same age: 60%, compared to 74%, in the 25–34 age group; 51%, compared to 69%, in the 34–44 age group; and 33%, versus 63%, in the 45–54 age group.

An estimated 6%[5] of the population of England is lesbian, gay, bisexual or transgender (LGBT); however, it is difficult to identify LGBT role models in sport. In some sports, it appears to be more accepted that women are openly lesbian, but men appear not to be accepted as readily if they are gay. This is particularly the case in team sports.

Active People

The Active People Survey measures adult participation in sport in England (defined as at least three 30-minute sessions of moderate activity per week). Results for the period 2010–2011 (APS5) show that:

- males are more likely to participate in sport than females

- non-white adults are marginally more likely to participate in sport than white adults

- people with a limiting disability or illness are significantly less likely to participate in sport.

Table 1: Percentage of people participating in sport

Variable	England
All adults	16.3%
Male	20.3%
Female	12.5%
White	16.2%
Non-white	17.2%
People with a limiting disability/illness	6.5%
People without a limiting disability/illness	18.0%

Results from the Active People Survey can be measured against baseline information collected in 2007/08. Statistically significant changes in this period include:

- a decline in participation among females

- a decline in the rate of participation among white adults

- an increase in the rate of participation among non-white adults.

[5] Source of statistics: Sport England (2000) *Making English Sport Inclusive: Equity Guidelines for Governing Bodies*. London: Sport England. Ref no: SE/1043/1M/6/00

People from disadvantaged communities

The statistics provided in the graph below (APS5 covering the 12-month period from April 2010 to April 2011) help to illustrate the gap in access to sports participation and coaching opportunities for disadvantaged communities.

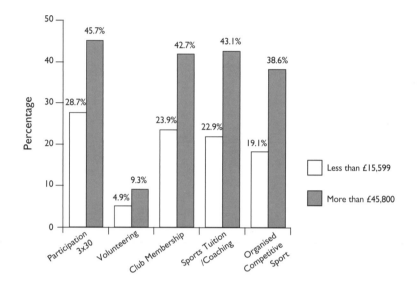

Figure 3: Participation in disadvantaged communities

It also provides a unique platform to promote StreetGames' core message that it is a 'supply side problem' and that latent demand among disadvantaged communities is greater than other social groups.

Coaches and sports providers need to work hard to provide activity at the right time, in the right place, at the right price and in the right style.

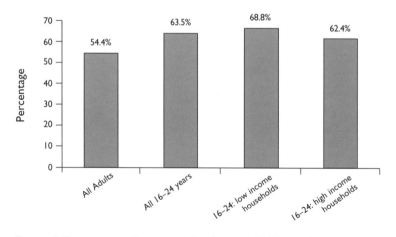

Figure 4: Percentage of young adults that would like to do more sport

Sports coaching in the UK

In 2008, sports coach UK carried out a survey of 10,000 adults on sports participation and coaching. This research found that the coaching workforce was not representative of the UK population in terms of gender, ethnicity, disability or socio-economic status.

Men are much more likely to be involved in coaching than women. 69% of those currently coaching are male (c 760,000) and 31% female (341,000). The gender inequality increases when coaching qualifications are considered: 82% of qualified coaches are male, with only 18% female.

In terms of ethnicity, the coaching workforce is under-representative of the UK adult population, especially for qualified coaches. 97% of all coaches and 99% of qualified coaches reported themselves as white, compared to 92% of the UK adult population.

Coaches with a limiting disability or illness are also likely to be under-represented. Only 8% of coaches have a limiting disability or illness, although this figure does rise to 11% of qualified coaches.

The current coaching population also massively over-represents those from higher socio-economic groups: 45% of coaches come from the highest rated socio-economic group, AB, compared to 26% of the UK adult population.

Local Demographics

It is important to recognise certain groups of people may be excluded from your sport, whether intentionally or not. Use national and, where relevant, regional and local population statistics as a guide to gauge how equitable your coaching sessions are. Marked regional variations can occur. For example, in 1996, the minority ethnic population in London was 26%, in the West Midlands 10% and in the South West 1%[6].

It is important to find out about the population statistics in your area. The following organisations should be able to provide relevant information:

- local council
- General Register Office for Scotland
- Northern Ireland Statistics and Research Agency
- Office for National Statistics (England and Wales).

1.4 Legal Requirements - An Overview

Providing sporting opportunities for everyone in society, regardless of their ability, ethnic group, gender, age, background, religion, belief or sexuality, is not just a moral responsibility, but could also be a legal requirement in some instances. This is particularly the case for organisations deemed to be service providers (eg local authorities, governing bodies of sport, sporting organisations).

By delivering coaching sessions, you are providing a service, but this does not necessarily classify you as the service provider in the eyes of the law. If you are employed by another party (eg a sports club), your employer is ultimately responsible for your actions. More often than not, it is the employer, not the employee, who is cited in employment tribunal/court cases. However, this should not be used as an excuse for inequitable practice on your part. You still have an important role to play in helping your employer respond positively to equality legislation and other equity-related initiatives. You may find yourself being asked to ensure, where possible, your coaching sessions are open and accessible to all sections of the community.

On the other hand, you may be one of the many coaches who work on a voluntary basis in a wide variety of situations and who receive little or no payment for their services and expertise, and little advice and support. Although the service you provide may not be subject to the same legal requirements as that of official service providers, it is still essential your coaching sessions are as equitable as possible and reflect best practice at all times.

Providing sporting opportunities for everyone, regardless of ability, ethnic group, gender, age, background, religion, belief or sexuality, is not just a moral duty, it is also a legal requirement.

[6] Source of statistics: Sport England (2000) *Making English Sport Inclusive: Equity Guidelines for Governing Bodies*. London: Sport England. Ref no: SE/1043/1M/6/00

The Equality Act was fully implemented in April 2011, consolidating much of the existing equality legislation in England, Scotland and Wales. This new legislation, however, is irrelevant in Northern Ireland, and the range of existing equality legislation related to gender, age, religion (unique to Northern ireland), disability and other protected characteristics remains in place.

Section Six will provide more detail on the Equality Act and its implications for you. In addition, the potential sources of liability that may affect you will be considered.

1.5 Summary

This section should have helped you understand the concept of sports equity and why it is so important. The key points you need to remember are listed in the panel below.

- The key element of sports equity is recognising inequalities (acknowledging certain groups of people are under-represented in all areas of sport). Understanding people's backgrounds will assist you in planning more effective coaching sessions.

- Many different groups of people are disadvantaged in sport. This will vary across the country as to which group. However, some groups experience discrimination on a more regular basis, not only in sport, but in their daily lives. This resource will, therefore, focus on the following protected characteristics:

    - disabled people

    - people from ethnic minorities

    - women and girls

    - people from economically disadvantaged backgrounds

    - people who follow different religions and beliefs

    - people of different ages

    - gay, lesbian, bisexual and transgender people.

- It is important to acknowledge, understand and adhere to equality legislation in the design and delivery of your coaching practice.

- Ensuring your coaching sessions are as accessible as possible means encouraging people from the protected characteristics to attend and enjoy the benefits of these sessions. To do this, it is important to understand why they might be discouraged from doing so. Section Two looks at the barriers that may prevent people from the protected characteristics participating in sport.

2.0 What's In It For You?

There are a variety of reasons why people could be put off attending your coaching sessions. This could be down to something either within or beyond your control. To ensure your coaching sessions are as accessible as possible, it is important to understand the barriers that might prevent people from the nine protected characteristics participating.

Some barriers to participation apply to everyone, not just people from the protected characteristics. These include:

- lack of awareness of sports activities on offer, due to poor, unsophisticated and untargeted marketing and promotion

- inconvenient times

- lack of spare time

- domestic/work commitments taking priority

- inconvenient venues

- poor facilities

- lack of transport

- fear for personal safety getting to and from the venue and, in some cases, at the venue

- expense of participation

- previous negative experiences (eg bad memories of physical education lessons at school)

- lack of motivation

- parental attitudes and influences.

However, some barriers are particularly relevant to people from the nine protected characteristics. This section is divided into subsections that deal with each of these characteristics in turn. By the end of the section, you should be able to:

- explain the barriers to participation for many of the nine protected characteristics

- identify the barriers to participation in specific coaching scenarios.

2.1 Disabled People

The following panel identifies the key issues that may act as barriers to disabled people participating in sport.

BARRIERS TO PARTICIPATION IN SPORT

Assumptions

- Don't assume that, just because not many disabled people currently attend your coaching sessions, they simply aren't interested in your sport.

- Don't assume disabled people just take part in sport because it's therapeutic. Disabled people participate in sport for the same reasons as non-disabled people (eg to improve fitness, make friends, as a personal challenge, for competition). The benefits of sport are also the same (eg improving confidence and self-esteem, handling pressure and stress).

- Don't make too many assumptions about whether people can take part in your sport – you'll be surprised how easily most sports can be adapted and how many disabled people can be successful with appropriate support from their coach.

- Coaching disabled people doesn't necessarily mean providing separate coaching sessions. It is often possible to integrate disabled people into existing sessions with players who may, or may not, be disabled.

- Assumptions about which sports disabled people are interested in.

- Assumptions about what disabled people can and cannot do.

- Assumptions that disabled people are wheelchair users only.

Lack of Informed Coaches

- Lack of coaches who are appropriately trained and informed about coaching disabled people.

- Lack of understanding among coaches about the different needs of people from different impairment groups.

- Lack of competitive opportunities.

Poor Communication

- Poor communication includes a failure to:

  - consult directly with disabled people to find out about their needs and aspirations

  - advertise sports opportunities for disabled people adequately and appropriately, and in places they regularly visit (eg day centres, special schools, youth clubs)

  - provide adequate encouragement. Some disabled people have low self-esteem and need more than just an advertisement to encourage them to take part in sport.

- Use of inappropriate language. Use common sense and language that isn't likely to offend disabled people – they will tell you if they are uncomfortable with your language.

Poor Facilities

- Lack of access to and within venues.

- Inadequate changing facilities.

- Lack of relevant and appropriate equipment.

Poor Timing

- Specific coaching sessions run at inconvenient times (eg off peak).

The following scenarios describe two different coaching situations. As you read through them, try to identify whether the organisation/coach could have done more to make the coaching sessions more accessible to disabled people.

Scenario 7

A local voluntary organisation wants to hold a 'come and try it' sports day for disabled people. They choose a venue because it is relatively cheap to hire for the day, although it is a bit out of the way on the outskirts of town and isn't on any major bus routes. They ask local sports clubs to hold hourly coaching sessions in their sport for any disabled people who turn up to the session.

The organisation sends letters to local schools and colleges, inviting disabled pupils to attend the 'come and try it' day and have a go at some of the activities on offer.

Stop and consider

Do you think the organisation would attract many disabled people to the 'come and try it' day? Why?

Scenario 8

A local leisure centre runs a judo club for young people every Tuesday evening. The club is both popular and successful, with many members doing well at local competitions.

Most club members attend a local school, where there are a number of disabled pupils. Several of the disabled pupils are keen to join the club, but because it is so popular, there are no places left for new members, disabled or otherwise.

Following consultation with potential new members, the club coach starts up a second club night at the leisure centre and divides new and existing members between the two nights, according to level of ability, not disability. Realising she will need help to run both club nights, she contacts members of the senior judo club to find out if anyone is interested in getting involved in coaching. She plans to encourage any coaches who come forward to work towards the British Judo Association (BJA) Level 2 Coaching Judo (if they've not already got it), and to attend the sports coach UK workshop 'Coaching Disabled Performers'.

Stop and consider

Do you think the judo coach would succeed in making her club accessible to disabled people? Why?

As you read through the feedback on the following page, try to relate it to your own situation and think about how you could make your coaching sessions more accessible to disabled people.

Scenario 7

The organisation would have been unlikely to attract many disabled people to the 'come and try it' day for the following reasons:

- Many people who were invited to the event might have been fed up with this kind of 'come and try it' day and would have preferred the opportunity to become a member of a sports club.

- Cost took priority over accessibility when the venue for the 'come and try it' day was selected. Because of this, it wasn't very easy for people to get to, which explains why attendance was far lower than expected.

- Not only was the venue difficult to get to in the first place, the building itself may not have catered particularly well for disabled people. For example:

  - no car park nearby

  - poor access and facilities for people in wheelchairs and with other mobility impairments

  - no hearing induction loops.

- Given the choice, the disabled pupils might have preferred to try different sports to those on offer.

- The organisers and coaches might not have been sufficiently trained or informed about coaching disabled people and, therefore, didn't take into account the different needs of people from various impairment groups.

- Appropriate equipment may not have been available.

Had the voluntary organisation consulted all the parties involved in the 'come and try it' day prior to making definite arrangements, many of the problems listed above could have been avoided. In addition, undertaking an audit process of the facility and site would have highlighted any particular issues that may have prevented anyone from the key target groups from being able to attend.

Scenario 8

The judo coach would have been likely to succeed in making her club accessible to disabled people for the following reasons:

- She arranged an additional club night, rather than just saying the club was full and couldn't accommodate any new members.

- She divided new and existing members between the two club nights by ability, not disability, rather than running separate club nights for non-disabled and disabled members.

- She consulted with potential members to indicate which would be the best night and time for the club night to take place.

- She contacted the senior judo club to identify potential new coaches to help her run the two club nights. Increasing the number of coaches at the club night would mean the coach:participant ratio is lower, and members would receive more individual attention.

- She planned to help senior judo club members work towards a recognised coaching qualification in judo. This would ensure all the club's coaches operate in line with the recommended good practice advocated by the BJA.

- She planned to arrange for all club coaches to receive training on coaching disabled people. This would ensure they understood the needs of club members who are disabled and were able to adapt their coaching methods to support them, where needed.

Points of Interest

The coach in Scenario 8 took positive steps to provide sporting opportunities for disabled people. The contrast with Scenario 7 should help you appreciate just how important it is to be organised, considerate and equitable in your coaching.

2.2 People from Minority Ethnic Communities

The following panel identifies the key issues that may act as barriers to people from minority ethnic communities participating in sport.

BARRIERS TO PARTICIPATION IN SPORT

Cultural/Religious Influences

- Religious beliefs – for example, it may not be possible to:

  - wear specified sports kit

  - attend coaching sessions during religious festivals or at times reserved for prayer.
    (See Appendix C for further information about religious festivals).

- Lack of single-gender coaching sessions with a coach of the appropriate gender.

- Lack of privacy in changing areas.

- Lack of parental support – in cases of 'traditional' families, Asian girls, in particular, may experience stricter parental control, which prevents them from participating in out-of-home leisure activities.

- Sport is often viewed as a **luxury** pastime, with little relevance to everyday life. Often, academic achievement or home-making responsibilities take precedence.

- Channelling of people into certain sports activities only – people from minority ethnic communities are often stereotyped as only being able to play certain sports, such as cricket or hockey.

Fear of Discrimination

- Fear of being discriminated against.

- Fear of racial abuse or attacks.

Low Self-esteem

- Lack of confidence and feeling self-conscious.

- Negative past experiences (eg at school).

- Having no-one to go with.

- Lack of positive images and role models.

Poor Communication

- Use of inappropriate language.

- Inadequate advertising of sports activities available in appropriate places (eg community centres).

Practicalities

- Cost.

- Lack of time.

- Lack of transport.

Unwelcoming Environment at Sports Centre

- Sports facilities are often seen as **mainstream** (ie for white communities).

- A feeling of not belonging.

- Unsympathetic and uninformed staff.

- Language barriers.

The following scenarios describe two different coaching situations. As you read through them, try to identify whether the coaches could have done more to make their coaching sessions more accessible to people from minority ethnic communities.

Scenario 9

A rugby coach decides to hold an open evening to encourage more young people from minority ethnic communities to join his club. He sets a date and produces the following flyer to advertise the event:

He distributes the flyer to local shops and the physical education department at the local comprehensive school, and leaves some at the club's reception.

Stop and consider

Do you think the rugby coach would attract many young people from minority ethnic communities to the open evening? Why?

COME AND HAVE A GO AT RUGBY JOIN OUR SCRUM!

WHEN?
Monday 21 September 2009

WHERE?
Anytown Rugby Club

TIME?
7–9pm

Scenario 10

A coach runs junior sessions at a hockey club. Most of the girls who attend the sessions come from outside the local area, and, although the coach doesn't have a problem with this, she also wants to encourage more local girls, most of whom are from minority ethnic communities, to take part. She contacts local community leaders for advice on how to do this. They provide her with the information she needs and give their seal of approval to her plans.

The coach produces a promotional flyer to advertise the hockey sessions and circulates it round the local community via schools, community centres, racial equality councils and community groups. The flyer contains:

- background information about the club

- details of the days and times when junior sessions are held

- details of the cost of coaching sessions and concessionary rates made available by the local authority leisure department

- a message of support from local community leaders.

The coach invites girls and their parents to come and watch one of the sessions and meet the other female coaches who help to run them. In addition, the coach employs a number of minority ethnic 'role models' to attend this initial session. She emphasises it isn't necessary to wear any particular kind of clothing or shoes to take part in the coaching sessions, as long as the clothes/shoes worn are comfortable, suitable and safe.

Stop and consider

Do you think the coach would attract many girls from minority ethnic communities to her hockey sessions? Why?

As you read through the feedback below, try to relate it to your own situation and think about how you could make your coaching sessions more accessible to people from minority ethnic communities.

Scenario 9

The rugby coach would have been unlikely to attract many young people from this protected characteristic to his open evening for the following reasons:

- He didn't liaise or consult with anyone from the local minority ethnic community about:

    – where the open evening was held

    – whether the date was suitable

    – whether the time was suitable

    – any other requirements people may have

    – the best way to promote the open evening.

    If he had, he would have found out that:

    – young people would have been more likely to go to the open evening if it had been held at the local community centre, rather than the usual club venue

    – the date clashed with Eid ul-Fitr, an important Muslim festival that would prevent some potential participants from attending the open evening

    – the communal changing facilities at the club would put people off

    – local community leaders could have advertised the open evening on his behalf. The fact they were supporting the event would have shown potential participants and their parents the club was serious about encouraging them to attend.

- He didn't explain that potential participants wouldn't need to wear special sports kit, or that all necessary equipment would be provided.

- He didn't provide any information about the coaches who would be running the open evening (ie whether there would be both male and female coaches present).

- He didn't include the cost (if any) of the open evening in his advert.

- The advert included a photo of a white rugby player. Using a photo of players from minority ethnic communities instead might have encouraged more people to attend the open evening.

- The open evening wasn't very well advertised.

Scenario 10

The coach would have been likely to succeed in making her hockey club accessible to all girls in the local area, regardless of ethnic origin, for the following reasons:

- She recognised that, although the majority of the girls in the local area are from minority ethnic communities, very few attend her hockey sessions.

- Rather than assume this was because they simply aren't interested in hockey, she realised many of them might either be unaware the hockey club existed, or would find it too daunting to join.

- She contacted local community leaders for advice on how to encourage girls from minority ethnic communities to attend her club, and got their seal of approval for her plan.

- She advertised the hockey sessions in places local girls regularly go to.

- She recognised the barriers that might prevent girls from minority ethnic communities attending the sessions and made sure the promotional flyer provided adequate reassurance:

    – She realised they might have never heard of the club, so she provided a bit of background information, together with the days and times of the junior sessions.

    – She kept the cost of the coaching sessions to a minimum and agreed concessionary rates with the local authority for people on low incomes.

    – She realised parents might be worried about allowing their daughters to attend the sessions, so she invited them to come along with their daughters to watch a session and meet the coaches.

– She realised that, due to religious or cultural reasons, it might not be appropriate for girls from minority ethnic communities to attend coaching sessions run by male coaches, so she ensured the sessions were run by female coaches.

– Similarly, she realised that, due to religious or cultural reasons, girls from minority ethnic communities might not be able to wear certain kinds of clothing, so she emphasised that they could wear whatever they liked, providing it was comfortable, suitable and safe.

– Her use of role models served to help motivate and inspire the girls and their parents as to what can be achieved.

Points of Interest

The coach in Scenario 10 took positive steps to provide sporting opportunities for girls from minority ethnic communities. The contrast with Scenario 9 should help you appreciate just how important it is to be equitable in your coaching practice.

2.3 Women and Girls

The following panel identifies the key issues that may act as barriers to women and girls participating in sport, regardless of their background. Many women will, of course, be members of more than one protected characteristic.

BARRIERS TO PARTICIPATION IN SPORT

Practical Barriers

- Lack of time.
- Lack of childcare.
- Lack of money.
- Lack of transport.
- Personal safety.
- Funding.
- Lack of access to facilities.
- Lack of female coaches.

Personal Barriers

- Body image.
- Clothing and equipment.
- Lack of self-confidence.
- Parental and adult influence.
- Peer-group pressure.

BARRIERS TO PARTICIPATION IN SPORT (continued)

Social and Cultural Barriers

• Male-dominated culture of sport.

• Lack of age- and stage-appropriate competition.

• Indifference or negative attitude of some sporting organisations towards some protected characteristics.

• Attitudes about sexuality.

• Attitudes about disability.

• Attitudes about ethnicity.

• Sexual harassment.

• Lack of role models, poor media coverage and provision of positive images of women and girls.

The following scenarios describe two different coaching situations. As you read through them, try to identify whether the coaches could have done more to make their coaching sessions more accessible to women and girls.

Scenario 11

Shiretown Leisure Centre is situated in the middle of a large industrial town. The centre was built about 20 years ago and has had the same manager all this time.

The centre is showing signs of wear and tear as the local authority have not had much money available to spend on it in recent years. A new leisure centre has been built on the outskirts of the town. It is modern and clean, with all the latest equipment and facilities, and a new, enthusiastic manager. The more forward-looking staff from the old centre have already got jobs at the new leisure centre, leaving the old centre short-staffed.

Tom is a self-employed football coach and is keen to encourage more women to play football. He decides to book the sports hall at the old leisure centre on Sunday evenings to run women's football sessions. He chooses the old leisure centre over the new one because it is cheaper and nearer to where he lives. He decides to run the sessions from 8–9pm as he is free at that time each week.

Tom designs a poster to advertise the football sessions (right).

Stop and consider

Do you think Tom would attract many women to his football sessions? Why?

Scenario 12

A cricket coach is specifically responsible for drawing up individually tailored training programmes for all new members at her club. She always meets new members individually and tries to make sure the training programmes she subsequently comes up with complement their lifestyle and other commitments. She also provides them with a list of essential equipment they will need and explains that, if they like, a more experienced cricketer will be assigned to them to provide guidance and support.

Her general approach is the same for both male and female athletes. She recognises that, generally, there are specific issues to bear in mind when preparing training programmes for female participants. However, she asks the same questions to both male and female members. These include:

- How many hours a week can you realistically devote to your training?
- When are the best times for you to train?
- How will you get to the club (eg own car, get a lift, public transport)?
- Training sessions may take place at other venues – would this be a problem?
- Would you prefer to attend mixed or women-/men-only training sessions?
- Would you prefer to attend training sessions run by a male or female coach?
- Would you be interested in using the club crèche?
- Do you have any other requirements?

Stop and consider

Do you think the cricket coach would succeed in making her club accessible to women?

As you read through the feedback below, try to relate it to your own situation and think about how you could make your coaching sessions more accessible to women and girls.

Scenario 11

Tom would have been unlikely to attract many women to his football sessions for the following reasons:

- Not many women were aware of the football sessions because they were only advertised at the leisure centre, which many had never been to before.
- The poster implied football is a male preserve.
- Tom assumed all women would jump at the chance of being able to play football when, in actual fact, they were more interested in other sports.
- The poster was offensive – this reflected badly on Tom both as a man and a coach, and several women decided that, although they quite fancied having a go at football, they didn't want to be coached by him.
- The poster didn't mention how much the sessions cost or whether equipment would be provided.

- The time of the session wasn't particularly convenient for most women.
- Many women didn't like being in the centre of town at that time of night.
- Public transport was practically non-existent on Sunday evenings.
- The leisure centre doesn't have a very welcoming environment:
  - The changing rooms aren't very clean.
  - There are no separate changing cubicles or showers.
  - The car park is badly lit at night.
  - The leisure centre manager isn't particularly welcoming or enthusiastic.
  - The leisure centre staff are overworked and less attentive to their customers.
  - There are no childcare facilities.

Scenario 12

The cricket coach would have been likely to succeed in making her club accessible to all, especially women, for the following reasons:

- She treated all new male and female club members equally. Women might be particularly reassured by the fact they didn't need to fork out for lots of new equipment straightaway and that they had the opportunity to receive guidance from a more experienced cricketer.

- In addition, she realised there are special issues to consider when devising training programmes for women and, therefore, found out as much as she could about their requirements beforehand. It is important to note she did not disenfranchise men, giving them the same opportunity to express their views. She took time to find out:

  - how much time both men and women could devote to training and what the best times to train were; women may often have other work, caring and/or domestic commitments that have to take priority, so it is important training times are convenient

  - how they would get to the club and made them aware training sessions might be held at different venues, as it is important all venues are convenient and safe to get to

  - whether they would prefer to attend mixed or women-/men-only training sessions led by male or female coaches; some women and men might feel more comfortable at sessions run by a female or male coach

  - whether it would help if a crèche was available at the time of the training sessions, as this might be an important factor that influences women, especially, to continue their membership of the club

  - whether they had any other requirements, as it is important the training programme caters for these.

Points of Interest

The coach in Scenario 12 took positive steps to provide sporting opportunities for women. The contrast with Scenario 11 should help you appreciate just how important it is to be equitable in your coaching practice.

2.4 People of Different Ages

The following panel identifies the key issues that may act as barriers to people of different ages participating in sport.

BARRIERS TO PARTICIPATION IN SPORT

Attitudes of Others

- Preconceptions about what people of different ages can achieve or do.
- Peer-group pressure.
- Lack of older or younger people being involved as participants or administrators.

Inconvenient Venue

- Lack of transport.
- Fear for personal safety getting to and from the venue.

Other Commitments

- School commitments have to take priority.
- Family commitments for older people.
- Too many conflicting interests.

Low Self-esteem

- Lack of confidence.
- Low expectations.
- Never undertaken different sports before.
- No friends to take part with.

Poor Communication

- People of different ages not contacted.
- Poor media coverage of older people doing sport.
- Poor and non-reflective positive imagery.

The following scenarios describe two different situations. As you read through them, try to identify whether the clubs could have done more to make their activities more accessible to people of different ages.

Scenario 13

A tennis club has a large membership of all ages, which includes both males and females. The club publishes its annual tournament programme and has age groups up to 30 years of age, before grouping all those over 30 years together. The competition committee decides, as the future of the club is with the juniors, it will group the older ages together with both men and women in the same group, so as to give more time to all the junior tournaments. The committee decides the over-30s tournament should only be played over one set – again, to leave more time for the three-set junior tournaments.

The junior tournaments are very successful and take up most of the day, and the club attracts new members in the junior section. The winners of the over-30s competitions are male and in their early 30s, having easily beaten the rest of the group.

Players over the age of 45 are told their role is to support the tournaments by being umpires and line judges.

Stop and consider

Do you think this will encourage more people over the age of 30 to join the club? Why?

Scenario 14

A rugby club has an active mini-rugby section on a Sunday morning, but is short of volunteers, as three parents do all the kit washing, setting out of the pitch and organising of equipment, such as balls and other training aids.

The volunteer coordinator identifies specific roles for each person within the mini-rugby section in helping to set out the pitch, and encourages two young people to take photographs and arrange for permissions to be gained and articles to go in the local press.

The volunteer coordinator arranges informal coach/team manager sessions for parents, as well as arranging an over-50s tag-rugby competition at the end of each Sunday session.

The three parents have a team of helpers and feel they are being supported by people of different ages.

Stop and consider

Do you think the club will increase the number of volunteers of different ages? Why?

As you read through the feedback below, try to relate it to your own situation and think about how you could make your coaching sessions more accessible to people of different ages.

Scenario 13

The club would have been unlikely to attract more people of an older age for the following reasons:

- It assumed everyone over the age of 30 is at the same level of fitness and ability.

- It assumed members over the age of 30 do not want to have any challenging competition.

- The competition committee assumed people are only interested in junior competitions.

- The committee didn't consult with members over the age of 30 about the tournament.

- The committee assumed young people could not umpire and be line judges, and that this is an older person's role.

- The committee assumed the longer game is suited to young people, and the older group cannot cope with more than one set.

- The committee did not give equal time to all age groups to enable a suitable conclusion.

Clearly, the older age groups were marginalised in favour of focusing upon the junior competitions.

Scenario 14

The club would have been likely to succeed and increase the number of volunteers from different age ranges for the following reasons:

- It took positive action to encourage young people to take key volunteer roles.

- It provided a modified game to make the sport attractive to people of different ages.

- It involved all ages in the development of new activities, which, in turn, will promote a greater loyalty to the club and its activities.

Points of Interest

The volunteer coordinator in Scenario 14 took positive steps to provide sporting opportunities for people of different ages. The contrast with Scenario 13 should help you appreciate just how important it is to be equitable in your coaching practice.

2.5 Economically Disadvantaged People

The following panel identifies the key issues that may act as barriers to people from economically disadvantaged backgrounds participating in sport.

BARRIERS TO PARTICIPATION IN SPORT

Attitudes of Others

- Preconceptions about the challenges people with economic disadvantages face.
- Lack of understanding.
- Peer-group pressure.
- Cost of activity.
- Lack of local coaches/leaders to run sessions – can the coach relate to participants?
- Image of a particular sport.
- Does the coach understand young people's motivations to participate? (These might not even relate to sport).

Inconvenient Venue

- Lack of affordable transport.
- Cost of the venue.
- Lack of suitable local activities/facilities – can young people access a sport in their neighbourhood, and do they feel they can travel their safely?

Low Self-esteem

- Lack of confidence.
- Low expectations.
- No friends to take part with.
- Lack of role models.
- Lack of right kit.

The following scenarios describe two different situations. As you read through them, try to identify whether the coach/club could have done more to make their activities more accessible to economically disadvantaged people.

Scenario 15

James is a community volleyball coach and has decided to enter an under-16 team in the local league, playing home and away in the region. The team of under 16s is selected from two inner-city schools at which James has coached. He arranges a minibus and for the players to meet in the city centre ahead of away games. He also arranges two sessions of two hours each week: one for games and one for training at the local leisure centre, which is on a train route, with a train due every half hour. The local leisure centre is not, however, on a bus route. The centre charges junior rates of £40 for the session, as the players are under 16 years of age.

James tells the players they must cover the cost of the court hire for both sessions, as, when they have a game, the away team doesn't pay for any court hire or officials. For the 10 players, this amounts to £4 per session. For away games, the local authority will pay petrol for the minibus and the players will be dropped off after the evening games in the city centre.

Stop and consider

Do you think James will be able to maintain the team throughout the season? Why?

As you read through the feedback below, try to relate it to your own situation and think about how you could make your coaching sessions more accessible to people from economically disadvantaged backgrounds.

Scenario 15

The team would have been unlikely to succeed for the following reasons:

- It was too costly for the players to maintain this level of financial commitment.

- The coach was on his own and likely to find it difficult to make sure players were able to keep going through the season.

- The leisure centre was a very expensive option for playing indoor team sports – a partnership with one of the schools may have been a better option.

- The coach assumed the players, although committed to the sport, would be able to find the money.

- The coach assumed the players felt safe to meet, and be dropped off, in the city centre.

Scenario 16

StreetGames' experience and research identify the following success factors for retention of players and continued participation:

- Building a sense of ownership and belonging.

- Collective decisions are made and stuck to.

- Group discipline is enforced by reference to the ground rules the group has set.

- Important people visit the project and increase the feeling of pride among participants.

- The progression route in the programme is attractive.

- The programme builds identity through giveaways (eg T-shirts and other branded goods).

- Young leaders are identified and democratic opportunities provided.

- Volunteering is an important aspect of the programme.

- Talented or keen participants are encouraged to make progress.

- The session is a safe place where young people can feel relaxed.

- It is not all sport – people want to have fun with their mates.

- The coach knows what participants want from the programme – in sporting and social senses.

- There are high points in the calendar (eg trips, away games, competitions).

- A sense of representing their neighbourhood is instilled via competitions and events.
- Participants go to new places, see new things and meet new people.
- The coach is a trusted adult.
- The coach is a role model.
- It is the best night of the week.

- The coach is the centre of the programme.
- The coach listens to young people and knows when to call in outside advice and when to refer them elsewhere.

It is important to note the issue of sustainability often arises when subsidised activity is being provided. Where possible, long-term agreements for subsidies should be secured, as well as exploring further options for grant aid.

Points of Interest

The club in Scenario 16 took positive steps to provide sporting opportunities for people from economically disadvantaged backgrounds. The contrast with Scenario 15 should help you appreciate just how important it is to be equitable and consider the personal circumstances of your coaching practice.

2.6 Lesbian, Gay, Bisexual and Transgender People

The following panel identifies the key issues that may act as barriers to lesbian, gay, bisexual and transgender people participating in sport.

BARRIERS TO PARTICIPATION IN SPORT

Practical Barriers
- Lack of appropriate changing facilities and toilets providing privacy for transgender participants.
- Lack of money for some female participants.
- Lack of investment in lesbian, gay, bisexual and transgender sport.

Attitudes of Others
- Preconceptions about the masculinity of gay and bisexual men and about the subsequent ability of gay and bisexual men to excel in sport.
- Preconceptions about the appropriateness of lesbian, gay, bisexual and transgender people to work with children and young people.
- Assumptions that lesbians are welcomed in sport and so no effort needs to be made to grow the participation of lesbian and bisexual women or to ensure the satisfaction of their experience with sport.
- Fear that transgender participants are 'cheats' and that transgender women, in particular, are participating in sport to gain an unfair physical advantage.
- Assumptions by coaches that all participants are heterosexual, which puts lesbians, gay men and bisexual in the position of having to 'come out' if they want to be honest about who they are or make reference to their family/home lives.

Personal Barriers
- Fear of discrimination, particularly for those with previous experience of homophobic/transphobic bullying in sport.
- Lack of visible lesbian, gay, bisexual and transgender coaches and role models in sport.
- Fear of homophobic language (such as 'poof') being used by coaches to put down participants who do not excel in sport, whether they are perceived to be gay or not.
- Lack of awareness of opportunities.

The following scenarios describe two different situations. As you read through them, try to identify whether the bodies could hve done more to make their activities more accessible to lesbian, gay, bisexual and transgender people.

Scenario 17

Two multi-sports clubs, one for women and one for men, decide to amalgamate to save costs and share a ground. The clubs agree the new committee structure, with both men and women equally represented on the committee. It is agreed that each team at all levels should have two coaches. The club agrees to have joint junior coaching sessions on a Sunday morning.

The clubs are discussing the committee and coaching structure and one of the men's club representatives asks that only one lesbian coach be allowed in each team. He states the reason why, as they will not be allowed into the female changing room prior to, and after, a game, and that they should change in the female toilets, with the other coach supervising the team.

He also asks that the balance of women on each committee be a balance of heterosexual and lesbian women. When challenged by the women members, he also asks that lesbian coaches be supervised at all times, as this is a child protection issue.

Stop and consider

Do you think the clubs will succeed in their amalgamation? Why?

Scenario 18

A governing body of sport is seeking to promote a new competition to recruit new members to different clubs in a particular local area. The governing body advertises in the local newspapers, on local radio and also uses different forms of media, modifying its website for people with a sight impairment. It also contacts the local gay and lesbian support groups, which recommend various media outlets to promote the new competition. The governing body changes its equity policy to take into account the Employment Equality (Sexual Orientation) Regulations 2003, recognising the need not to discriminate against lesbian, gay, bisexual and transgender people.

The governing body has entered a team in the International Gay and Lesbian Games, drawn from different teams across the country. This is promoted in the governing body magazine and the results celebrated on the website.

Stop and consider

Do you think the governing body will increase the number of lesbian, gay, bisexual and transgender people taking part in the sport? Why?

Scenario 17

The clubs would have been unlikely to succeed in their amalgamation for the following reasons:

- The men's committee discriminated against the women's selection.

- The men's committee made assumptions about the women's membership.

- The men's committee had responded to peer pressure.

- Coaches' sexuality was not an issue. All coaches – male, female, heterosexual, gay, lesbian, bisexual or transgender – would have gone through the appropriate child protection checks in order to coach young people.

Scenario 18

The governing body would have been likely to succeed and increase the number of young people participating in local clubs for the following reasons:

- It actively promoted a positive image of lesbian, gay, bisexual and transgender people.

- It had no preconceptions about anybody.

- It allocated resources to support specific entry into competition.

Points of Interest

The governing body in Scenario 18 took positive steps to provide sporting opportunities for lesbian, gay, bisexual and transgender people. The contrast with Scenario 17 should help you appreciate just how important it is to be equitable and consider the personal circumstances of your coaching practice.

2.7 Faith-based Groups and Communities

The following panel identifies the key issues that may act as barriers to people from faith-based groups and communities participating in sport.

BARRIERS TO PARTICIPATION IN SPORT

Attitudes of Others

- A lack of awareness of faith-based festivals.

- A lack of awareness of periods of religious obligation and/or observance of religious beliefs.

- A lack of awareness of dietary restrictions.

- A lack of awareness of historical and cultural issues that affect attitudes in some cultures and the cultural traits of certain groups.

- A lack of awareness of the needs of different faith-based groups and the understanding of specific faith and cultural restrictions, including clothing, food and drink, physical contact and other requirements.

- A lack of consultation with local community groups.

Personal Barriers

- Body image.

- Clothing and equipment.

- Lack of self-confidence.

- Parental and adult influence.

- Peer-group pressure.

Many of the barriers experienced by the other protected characteristics are, of course, also relevant to this particular protected characteristic.

The following scenario highlights a situation where no thought has been given to protected characteristics as part of the planning process. As you read through this scenario, try to identify whether the chief executive could have done more to make the funding process accessible to all communities.

Scenario 19

The chief executive of a coaching agency promotes and invites applications from all communities to put on coaching activities in a variety of sports, claiming an open and transparent process for accepting and selecting beneficiary applicants. The criteria for accessing the funding stream states applicant individuals and organisations should:

- be not-for-profit

- be able to match the funding by 50%

- ensure that any activities organised as a result of funding secured take place in the months of August and September 2009.

Stop and consider

Do you think the coaching agency will attract applicants from Muslim individuals and groups?

Scenario 19

Clearly, this has not been thought through in order to attract applications from all communities. There is a real chance members of the Muslim community will not apply because:

- statistics show voluntary groups from a minority ethnic community are less likely to be able to access funds from other grants and funding streams; hence, their confidence will be low in any similar processes

- these same groups are less likely to be able to match funding for any applications

- the months of August and September 2009 coincide with the months of Ramadan for Muslims – a very important time of the year. The month of Ramadan is a time for spiritual reflection, prayer, doing good deeds and spending time with family and friends. The fasting is intended to help teach Muslims self-discipline, self-restraint and generosity. It also reminds them of the suffering of the poor, who may rarely get to eat well. It is common to have one meal just before sunrise and another directly after sunset. Consequently, Muslims are much less likely to organise or indeed indulge in physical activity during this month.

Note that the date of the month of Ramadan changes each year. In 2010, Ramadan will be starting around 12 August. You need to be aware of when Ramadan is happening as part of good practice when planning. Information is available from the Shap Working Party, a group that produces a religious festival calendar each year to cover all the main religions of the world.

Many of the principles outlined in Scenario 19 should also be followed when organising activities for this protected characteristic.

2.8 Summary

Although certain barriers to participation apply only to a specific protected characteristic, you will have noticed many are common to all the other characteristics. The figure on the next page should help you to remember what these are.

Those involved in Scenarios 8 (page 13), 10 (page 17), 12 (page 22), 14 (page 25), 16 (page 28) and 18 (page 30) made every effort to be fair to everyone who wanted to be involved in their sport. This meant additional and specific effort in some areas (eg arranging an additional judo club night) and relaxing rules in others (eg allowing girls at the netball club to wear whatever clothing they felt most comfortable in). In all scenarios, this may have resulted in more people being involved in sport.

You should aim to put the same effort and application into your coaching practice. To further support your inclusive coaching practice, Section Three looks at the appropriate language and terminology to use when talking or referring to the protected characteristics.

SPORT

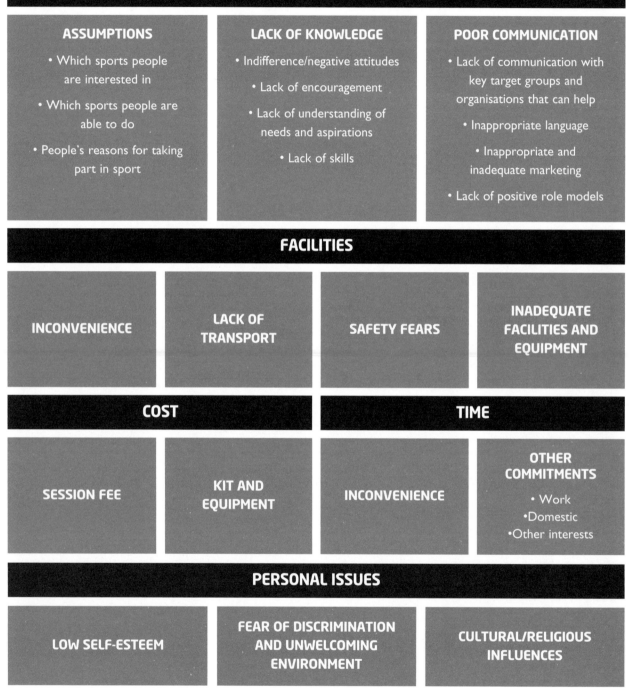

COACH

ASSUMPTIONS

- Which sports people are interested in
- Which sports people are able to do
- People's reasons for taking part in sport

LACK OF KNOWLEDGE

- Indifference/negative attitudes
- Lack of encouragement
- Lack of understanding of needs and aspirations
- Lack of skills

POOR COMMUNICATION

- Lack of communication with key target groups and organisations that can help
- Inappropriate language
- Inappropriate and inadequate marketing
- Lack of positive role models

FACILITIES

| INCONVENIENCE | LACK OF TRANSPORT | SAFETY FEARS | INADEQUATE FACILITIES AND EQUIPMENT |

COST

| SESSION FEE | KIT AND EQUIPMENT |

TIME

INCONVENIENCE

OTHER COMMITMENTS

- Work
- Domestic
- Other interests

PERSONAL ISSUES

| LOW SELF-ESTEEM | FEAR OF DISCRIMINATION AND UNWELCOMING ENVIRONMENT | CULTURAL/RELIGIOUS INFLUENCES |

PARTICIPATION

3.0 What's In It For You?

In any coaching situation, it is important to treat your participants fairly and with respect – language has a vital role to play in this. In order to create a positive, welcoming coaching environment, it is essential the language you use is:

- sensitive

- appropriate

- relevant

- consistent.

Language is continually evolving as awareness and attitudes change. For example, several words used in the context of disability, which were acceptable in the past, are now no longer used. **Spastic** used to be a common

term, but has now been replaced by **person with cerebral palsy**. This was mainly due to the misuse of the term, which subsequently became one of ridicule.

By the end of this section, you should be:

- aware of the appropriate terminology to use when referring to people from most of the protected characteristics, both during and outside your coaching sessions

- able to identify examples of acceptable and unacceptable terminology.

The information in this section is by no means exhaustive, nor a definitive guide. The terms included here may, in due course, be revised, or may disappear in the future and be replaced by other terms.

3.1 Disabled People

The following table contains some of the common terms associated with disability. The left-hand column lists terms used in the past, which should now be avoided; the right-hand column lists more acceptable alternatives. Some of the terms are also mentioned in Appendix D (page 137).

Unacceptable	Acceptable
the blind	partially sighted people/visually impaired people
the deaf/hard of hearing/profoundly deaf	deaf people or people with a hearing impairment
deaf and dumb	people with a hearing impairment and without speech
the disabled/the handicapped/cripples/invalids	disabled people
disabled toilets	accessible toilets
dumb/mute	person with a speech impairment/ speech-impaired person
an epileptic	person with epilepsy
handicap	disability/impairment
mentally disabled/subnormal/abnormal/ retarded/backward	person with learning disabilities
Mongolism	Down's syndrome
normal people/able-bodied people	non-disabled people
patient	person
spastic	person with cerebral palsy
special needs	(additional or individual) needs
wheelchair bound/confined to a wheelchair	wheelchair user
wheelchair coach	coach
victim of/stricken by/crippled by/afflicted by/sufferer of	has/with (the particular condition)

3.2 People from Minority Ethnic Communities

As with terms relating to disability, many of those associated with people from minority ethnic communities should be avoided, even if they were regarded as acceptable in the past. Examples include:

Term	Reasons to Avoid	Acceptable
Chink	Used to refer to people of perceived Chinese descent. Describes their eye slits or chinks. Considered extremely derogatory[7].	A Chinese person
Coconut	Term used to denounce another who is of black or brown heritage, but not reflecting the perceived values of the black or brown community (ie 'black on the outside, white on the inside')[7].	A black and minority ethnic person
Coloured	Regarded as outdated and generally offensive to many black people. When applied to South Africa, the term reflects issues of ethnic divide and apartheid[8].	A black and minority ethnic person
Half-caste	Regarded as outdated and racist. Implies 'half a person'[8].	Mixed race or now, increasingly, 'dual heritage'
Nigger	An offensive and derogatory term used by white people towards black people during the slave trade in the southern states of the USA. Sometimes used now in black rap songs, as a term between one black person and another. Use of the word is often perceived as extremely offensive if used by a white person in any context[7].	A black African American person
Non-white	Implies that white is the generic term for all people[8].	A black and minority ethnic person
Paki	An offensive and derogatory term often used to refer to people from Pakistan, or Asian people in general[8].	A person from Pakistan

[7] Adapted from Google Dictionary.

[8] Taken from the British Sociological Association website (www.britsoc.co.uk).

You should always use acceptable terminology when referring to people from minority ethnic communities. The most common terms you need to be aware of include:

Term	Guidance
Asian people	Use this term when referring to people from China, India, Pakistan, Bangladesh and Sri Lanka. Bear in mind that some people may prefer to refer to their country of origin (eg Bangladeshi, Indian, Pakistani), rather than to the general term Asian, which includes a wide variety of different cultural and ethnic groups. Other people may prefer to be referred to neither as Asian nor by their country of origin if several generations of their family have been living in Britain[9]. Note that South Asian is a term that includes people from India, Pakistan, Bangladesh and Sri Lanka.
Black people	Use this term when referring to African, Caribbean and some Asian people. However, remember that some Asian groups in Britain object to being referred to as **black**. Some people believe the term confuses a number of ethnic groups, which should be treated separately. One solution to this is to refer to **black peoples or black communities** in the plural, to imply there is a variety of such groups. You should also be aware that **black** can also be used in a racist sense in certain contexts[9].
People from black and minority ethnic communities	Use this term when referring collectively to people of different ethnic origins and backgrounds who are not white and are a minority. Indeed, Asians living in Leicester will soon be a majority (as will the black and Asian communities in Birmingham).

A more detailed list of terminology associated with people from minority ethnic communities is provided in Appendix E.

[9] Based on information provided on the British Sociological Association website (www.britsoc.co.uk).

3.3 Women and Girls

Although often unintentional, many people refer or talk to women and girls using terms sometimes perceived as patronising and offensive. The table below shows some of the terms to avoid, together with more acceptable alternatives.

Context	Avoid	Use
Referring/talking to a group of female participants	Birds/chicks/girls/ladies	Everyone/everybody/ women/females
Referring/talking to an individual female participant	Bird/chick/dear/duck/love/pet	Name the participant wants to be known by/woman/female
Referring to the appropriate senior individual within an organisation	Chairman	Chair/chairperson
Sports environment	You throw/run/tackle/hit like a girl	Do not use the female gender to criticise participants
Office environment	Girls in the office	Staff/office staff
Office environment	Manpower	Workforce/staff/employees
Office environment	Manning	Staffing
Office environment	Man hours	Hours worked
Office environment	Man management	People management

Not everyone will find the terms in the Avoid column patronising and offensive – some people may be quite happy for you to use them. Use your discretion when talking or referring to women and girls in your coaching sessions. If in doubt, ask participants how they would prefer to be addressed.

3.4 People of Different Ages

Although often used in jest or as a compliment, the identification of age can sometimes demonstrate a perception that a particular group or individual cannot carry out a particular activity.

People over the age of 20 are likely to live more than 20 years longer than their parents due to advances in medical treatment, diet and lifestyle. Therefore, decisions should be made on the basis of ability rather than age. The same goes for young people, as well as mature people, and the expectations of younger people should not be prejudiced by assumptions about a particular age group.

So, the term 'people of different ages' is acceptable. Not acceptable are 'the elderly' or 'the aged' – instead, use the term 'older people'.

3.5 Economically Disadvantaged People

The identification of people regarded as economically disadvantaged is very difficult, as many people from other groups can also fall into this category – especially disabled people, black and minority ethnic people, some faith groups and also women. Many factors may lead to people being economically disadvantaged.

These include:

- where they live (both urban and rural)
- health problems
- their status as refugees and asylum seekers
- those at risk of offending, offenders and ex-offenders
- whether or not they are old
- whether or not they have a disability
- if they are young people at risk
- if they are living in poverty
- if they are unemployed.

The Indices of Multiple Deprivation (IMD) provide a ranking of areas across the country according to their level of deprivation, taking into consideration key factors such as income, employment, health and disability, education, skills and training, barriers to housing and services, living environment and crime.

The link below provides relevant information for England. There are also similar sites for Scotland and Wales.

www.communities.gov.uk/corporate/researchandstatistics/
statistics/subject/indicesdeprivation

3.6 Lesbian, Gay, Bisexual and Transgender People

Homophobia is a fear of and/or hostility towards gay people or homosexuality. Homophobia is often expressed visibly, audibly and sometimes violently. Research carried out in 1996 by gay rights group Stonewall showed gay people had experienced more extreme homophobia as young people than as adults. The research found, as young people, 90% of the respondents had been called names and nearly 50% had been violently attacked.

Homophobic and transphobic language is language that implies that because someone is lesbian, gay, bisexual or transgender, they are somehow inferior. In sport, as in wider society, homophobic and transphobic language is often used to refer to people who are not, or not perceived to be, lesbian, gay, bisexual or transgender. They are terms of abuse used to put people down.

Language

Avoid labels such as:

- lezzer
- dyke
- poof
- faggot
- batty boy
- gay boy
- queer
- sissy.

Avoid expressions such as:

- 'playing like a girl'
- 'playing like a poof'
- 'get up, you girl's blouse'
- 'that's so gay'
- 'that's so bent'.

Use the correct terminology to refer to lesbian, gay, bisexual and transgender people:

- lesbian or gay woman
- gay man
- bisexual (bisexual woman or man)
- transgender (the abbreviation 'trans', as in 'trans person' is also acceptable).

3.7 Summary

You should now be familiar with which terms to use and which to avoid when talking or referring to people from the protected characteristics. The next activity asks you to identify examples of acceptable and unacceptable terminology.

ACTIVITY 2

The table below contains a number of statements about people from the protected characteristics. Decide whether each statement is acceptable and write **Yes** or **No** in the second column. If a statement is not acceptable, write a more acceptable alternative in the third column.

	Statement	Acceptable?	More Acceptable Alternative (if appropriate)
1	Harpal runs coaching sessions for both able-bodied and disabled gymnasts.		
2	Tony is a swimming coach, aiming to encourage more non-white people in the local area to take up swimming.		
3	Sophie contacts her governing body to find out more about coaching participants suffering from Down's syndrome.		
4	Matthew makes sure his coaching venue has accessible toilets for wheelchair users.		
5	Daniel is asked to coach a women's rugby team. He declines, saying he 'doesn't think rugby is a bird's game'.		
6	Nawal is asked to start coaching a group of mentally disabled teenagers who are interested in taking up badminton.		
7	Hassiba runs basketball coaching sessions at her local community centre specifically aimed at women and girls from black and Asian communities.		
8	Desmond contacts British Blind Sport for information on modifying sports for visually impaired people.		
9	Carla is a wheelchair tennis coach.		
10	'OK, Sandra – can you return to your half of the court and prepare to serve again?' said the squash coach.		
11	Steve said Bob was 'playing like a gay'.		

Feedback

	Statement	Acceptable?	More Acceptable Alternative (if appropriate)
1	Harpal runs coaching sessions for both able-bodied and disabled gymnasts.	NO	• Harpal runs coaching sessions for both **non-disabled** and **disabled athletes**. • Harpal runs coaching sessions for **gymnasts of all abilities**.
2	Tony is a swimming coach, aiming to encourage more non-white people in the local area to take up swimming.	NO	• Tony is a swimming coach, aiming to encourage more **people from local minority ethnic communities** to take up swimming.
3	Sophie contacts her governing body to find out more about coaching participants suffering from Down's syndrome.	NO	• Sophie contacts her governing body to find out more about coaching participants **who have/with** Down's syndrome.
4	Matthew makes sure his coaching venue has accessible toilets for wheelchair users.	YES	• It is appropriate to refer to **accessible toilets** and **wheelchair users**.
5	Daniel is asked to coach a women's rugby team. He declines, saying he 'doesn't think rugby is a bird's game'.	NO	• Not only is Daniel wrong to refer to women as 'birds', but he is also wrong to suggest women cannot and should not play rugby!
6	Nawal is asked to start coaching a group of mentally disabled teenagers who are interested in taking up badminton.	NO	• Nawal is asked to start coaching a group of teenagers **with learning disabilities**.
7	Hassiba runs basketball coaching sessions at her local community centre specifically aimed at women and girls from black and Asian communities.	YES	• It is appropriate to refer to **black and Asian communities**.
8	Desmond contacts British Blind Sport for information on modifying sports for visually impaired people.	YES	• It is appropriate to refer to **visually impaired people**.
9	Carla is a wheelchair tennis coach.	NO	• Carla is a **tennis** coach.
10	'OK, Sandra – can you return to your half of the court and prepare to serve again?' said the squash coach.	YES	• It is appropriate to address any participant by the name by which they wish to be known.
11	Steve said Bob was 'playing like a gay'.	NO	• As a coach, Steve should not be using negative phrases. He should use a constructive approach to build self-esteem.

Remember!

- Use language that is sensitive, appropriate and relevant.

- Conversation between friends is different to a conversation with people you don't know well.

- If you are unsure which terms are acceptable or unacceptable, ask the people you are coaching.

- Everybody has the right to choose how they wish to be referred to – not everyone may choose to be referred to in the same way.

- If people refer to themselves in a way you find offensive, you don't have to use that word just because they do.

Using appropriate language and terminology is just one way of ensuring your coaching sessions are as equitable as possible. Section Four looks at ways of applying and extending your existing coaching skills and experience to meet the needs of your participants.

ACTIVITY 4

Read through the following scenario. As you do, try to identify the ways in which Kath makes her coaching scheme accessible and appropriate for women and girls from minority ethnic communities, and list them in the space provided on the next page.

Scenario 21

Kath is a coach at a local rowing club. She realises very few women and girls from minority ethnic communities are members of her club and wants to do something to encourage more to take up rowing.

She arranges to meet with local community leaders to discuss her plan. In particular, she asks them about the barriers that might discourage women and girls from joining the club (eg cost, transport, time of coaching sessions, equipment required) and the best way to advertise the coaching scheme she intends to launch. The local community leaders think Kath's scheme is a great idea and say they will do everything they can to help her. They also indicate the dates and times when it would not be convenient to run the sessions. They put Kath in touch with a black female rower from the local area to feature as a positive role model in the promotional material she intends to produce.

Kath decides to run two sets of coaching sessions: one at the local community centre for those who would rather have a go at rowing on dry land before venturing on to the water, and the other at a local lake for those who would rather go straight out on to the water. She enlists the help of other coaches from her rowing club, including two female coaches.

She produces a promotional flyer to advertise the coaching scheme, which includes the following information:

- details of the two sets of coaching sessions on offer (ie one on dry land, the other on the water) with a note explaining potential participants are free to swap to the other scheme after the introductory session, should they wish

- details of the date, time and venue of the first sessions

- information about the cost of the coaching sessions – the first one will be free and subsequent ones heavily subsidised

- details of free transport available to and from the coaching venues

- the names of the female coaches who will be helping Kath to run the two schemes

- reassurance that all necessary equipment will be provided – all potential participants need to bring is themselves!

- reassurance that no special kit needs to be worn – as long as it's suitable and safe for rowing, potential participants may wear whatever they feel most comfortable in

- a message of encouragement from the local community leaders and local black female rower.

Kath distributes the promotional flyers via routes identified by local community leaders (eg local community centres, inserted in local community free newspaper).

Stop and consider

How does Kath make her coaching scheme accessible and appropriate for women and girls from minority ethnic communities? List the ways in the space provided on the next page.

Feedback

Kath made her coaching sessions as equitable as possible by:

- identifying that very few women and girls from minority ethnic communities were members of her rowing club and deciding to do something to encourage more to take up rowing

- meeting and consulting with local community leaders to find out how best to tailor her rowing schemes to meet the needs of women and girls from minority ethnic communities

- using a positive role model

- using local facilities and providing free transport. The issue of sustainability often arises – Kath should secure longer-term commitment to this subsidy to ensure subsequent sessions are not affected

- trying to identify the most appropriate dates and times to run the coaching sessions, by asking community leaders

- providing free/subsidised coaching sessions

- enlisting the help of other female coaches from minority ethnic communities

- providing all necessary equipment

- having a relaxed dress code

- ensuring the promotional flyer included the kind of information women and girls from minority ethnic communities wanted to know

- publicising the support of local community leaders and the positive role model

- distributing the promotional flyers via appropriate routes.

4.3 Women and Girls

Don't Make Assumptions

- Don't assume that, just because not many women and girls currently attend your coaching sessions, they simply aren't interested in your sport. Think back to the barriers to participation identified in Section 2.3.

- Don't assume all women and girls are interested in the same kinds of activities. Offer as wide a choice as possible and tailor your coaching programmes to meet their different needs.

- Don't make assumptions about the capabilities of women and girls in your sport. All participants, regardless of gender, should be assessed individually to establish their current level of ability.

Communicate

- Consult women and girls to find out what sort of activities they are interested in (eg interviews, questionnaires).

- Use language that is sensitive, appropriate and relevant both during and outside your coaching sessions (see Section 3.3 for more information).

- Do not refer to a woman's marital status.

- Include positive images of women and girls in any promotional material you produce. Such material should reflect real women and girls in society, not just the model-like perfection frequently portrayed in women's magazines.

- Encourage other coaches at your club to attend the sports coach UK 'Equity in Your Coaching' workshop. Workshop dates and locations are available from the Workshop Booking Centre.

See page 108 for contact details of the Workshop Booking Centre.

Cater For Different Needs

- Understand the barriers that may discourage women and girls from participating in sport:

  - Many women and girls don't feel comfortable or confident at mixed sessions (eg fear of ridicule or abuse, don't want to look silly, being worried about their appearance).

  - Many women and girls underestimate their levels of competence in sport and may think they aren't experienced or good enough to join coaching sessions.

  - Personal safety is a particularly important issue for women and girls (eg transport, car-park lighting, access to venue, timing).

  - Barriers can sometimes be small things. Little adjustments to your sporting programme can make a big difference. Speak to your participants.

- Understand the legal requirements under which you practise. Under the terms of sex discrimination legislation, it is only acceptable to run women-only coaching sessions if:

  - female participants are likely to suffer serious embarrassment due to the presence of male participants

  - female participants are likely to be in a state of undress and might reasonably object to the presence of male participants

  - physical contact is likely with participants of the opposite sex, and women and girls might reasonably object to this

  - coaching sessions are run by a single-sex voluntary group

  - the session is designed to educate or train, and through monitoring information, you can show female participants are under-represented.

In all cases, you need to be able to justify running women-only sessions (eg expressed preferences from existing or potential participants, religious/cultural reasons, results of research/surveys). You may also need to restrict the running of coaching sessions to female coaches and consider allowing female spectators only, or perhaps no spectators at all.

- Take time to find out what the 'player pathway' is for females in your sport. This may mirror that of male counterparts, but there are some differences. If you are to support participants to achieve their full potential, you need to know where to direct them.

- Promote female athletes in your area as role models for girls at your club. Due to the relative lack of media coverage, there may be a perception that females can't aspire to high levels of performance in sport. Working with governing bodies of sport and county sports partnerships (CSPs) to address this issue through your club could help change this perception.

- There is also a relative lack of female coaches. By becoming the best coach you can be and ensuring all those you coach gain a positive experience, you could become a role model yourself and inspire the next generation of female sports coaches.

- Once you have attracted female participants to your club, it is important they feel welcome and part of the club. Wherever possible, engage them in the decision-making process. You can't do this on your own – work with other officers and members in the club to develop a positive and welcoming environment.

- Particularly for the younger participants, place the emphasis on the development of core skills in line with the long-term athlete development (LTAD) model. Competition has its place, but females are more likely to continue participating if they feel comfortable in their own skin. A lack of self-esteem often prevents them taking part. Focus on individual needs, allowing each individual to progress at their own pace.

- Be aware of the physiological differences between male and female participants of different ages that may affect performance (eg children's development, or conditions that specifically affect female participants, such as osteoporosis or menstruation).

- Ensure your coaching sessions are held at easily accessible and safe venues that provide a welcoming environment for women and girls, both in terms of staff and facilities.

- Consider including opportunities at the start and/or conclusion of your session for informal chats with participants.

- Although it may be difficult to find a time to suit everyone, establish the most convenient times for women to attend your coaching sessions. Women often have the same work commitments as men and, often, additional caring responsibilities, so don't automatically assume you can run women's sessions during weekday off-peak periods only.

- Consider the public transport links to your training venue and encourage carpooling. This will benefit women and girls who would otherwise have difficulty getting to the venue, as well as those who feel uncomfortable about travelling alone to coaching sessions.

- If your coaching venue doesn't already have one, consider providing a crèche for women bringing young children with them.

- Make sure your coaching sessions are reasonably priced, but remember that pricing policies must not discriminate between men and women. Female participants cannot be offered discounts that are not available to the same category of male participants. Consider 'pay and play' payment schemes as opposed to annual membership commitments.

- Consider alternatives to expensive equipment and kit (eg allowing a relaxed dress code).

Act Appropriately

- In order to create a positive, welcoming coaching environment, make sure you use language that is sensitive, appropriate and relevant, so as not to upset or offend women and girls. It can be difficult to know what is acceptable and unacceptable – refer back to Section Three for guidance.

- During mixed coaching sessions:

    - use both male and female participants to demonstrate new skills

    - match participants by skill, rather than gender, when dividing them into pairs or small groups to learn new skills

    - check participants feel comfortable about pair/group work with members of the opposite sex.

- As a general rule:

    - refrain from over-familiarity and respect participants' individual space

    - never make comments or remarks of a sexual nature

    - if some coaching techniques require physical contact or support, check your governing body of sport guidelines and ask the participant's permission first; touching can be okay and appropriate, as long as it is neither intrusive nor disturbing

    - avoid going into changing facilities, especially while participants are getting changed; if it cannot be avoided, always ask participants' permission first

    - avoid spending time alone with individual participants

    - avoid giving participants a lift to and from coaching sessions in your car, unless absolutely necessary, particularly if you are likely to be alone together.

Seek Advice

If in doubt, contact organisations that can offer help and advice.

See pages 119–133 for contact details.

Bear in mind the information on the preceding pages as you complete the next activity.

ACTIVITY 5

Read through the following scenario. As you do, try to identify the ways in which Jane makes her coaching sessions accessible and appropriate for both men and women, and list them in the space provided at the end of the scenario.

Scenario 22

Jane is a coach at a local cricket club. She decides to set up coaching sessions for beginners, which will be open to both men and women. She runs an introductory session to assess the existing skills of the participants. This includes drills and technique work in batting, bowling and fielding.

She starts off by observing the participants and later divides them into pairs, matching similarly skilled players, having first made sure the participants feel comfortable about working with members of the opposite sex.

When introducing new skills, Jane is as likely to ask a woman to demonstrate as she is to ask a man. She is sensitive in her use of language and uses both men and women as positive role models for particular coaching points.

Stop and consider

How does Jane make her coaching session accessible and appropriate for both male and female participants? List the ways in the space provided below.

....

....

....

....

....

....

....

....

....

4.4 People of Different Ages

Don't Make Assumptions

- Don't assume that, just because people are younger or older than the norm, they simply aren't interested in your sport. Think back to the barriers to participation identified in Section 2.4.

- Remember, the reasons people participate in sport are the same, regardless of age (eg for fun, to improve fitness, make friends, as a personal challenge, for competition). The benefits of sport are also the same (eg improving confidence and self-esteem, handling pressure and stress). Try to raise awareness of these benefits – if possible, use people of different ages as positive role models.

Communicate

- Consult with relevant organisations about issues such as:

    - appropriate venues, days and times for coaching sessions

    - specific requirements for people of different ages

    - appropriate means of advertising your coaching sessions.

    Doing this will prove to people of different ages that you are serious about encouraging them to join your coaching sessions.

- Use language that is sensitive, appropriate and relevant, both during and outside your coaching sessions (see Section 3.4 for more information).

- People of different ages will have different needs and aspirations. It is, therefore, important to consult with individuals to find out about:

    - any specific requirements

    - what kind of support they will need from you

    - existing skills and fitness levels

    - what they hope to achieve from coaching sessions

    - other issues (eg transport, costs).

    If you are coaching children and young people, don't forget to consult with their parents, to gain their support.

- Advertise your coaching sessions adequately and appropriately. Make sure any promotional material you produce includes information relevant to people of different ages.

- Encourage other coaches at your club to attend the sports coach UK 'Equity in Your Coaching' and 'Coaching Children and Young People' workshops. Workshop dates and locations are available from the Workshop Booking Centre.

See page 108 for contact details of the Workshop Booking Centre.

Act Appropriately

- In order to create a positive, welcoming coaching environment, make sure you use language that is sensitive, appropriate and relevant, so as not to upset or offend people of different ages. It can be difficult to know what is acceptable and unacceptable – refer back to Section Three for guidance.

Seek Advice

If in doubt, contact organisations that can offer help and advice.

See pages 119–133 for contact details.

Bear in mind the information on the preceding page as you complete this activity.

ACTIVITY 6

Read through the following scenario. As you do, try to identify the ways in which Peter makes his coaching sessions accessible and appropriate to people of different ages, and list them in the space provided at the end of the scenario.

Scenario 23

Peter is a multi-sports coach in a rural community and is having difficulty getting enough people of different age groups to reach a critical mass to engage in a number of different activities.

He consults with local schools, different community groups and associations, and plans a fun event in a local park with local coaches providing the lead for each session. He brings in clubs from different sports, including walking, cycling, angling and karate. He organises softball himself, encouraging families and street groups to take part together.

He promotes incentives to the event in local groups, community associations and shops, aimed at families and street groups.

He finds that family groups take part in different activities, and a number of the clubs gain new members, including a group of young people who would like to do BMX cycling, as well as road cycling.

The family/street softball event is a great success and is planned to be played every month during the summer.

Stop and consider

How does Peter make his coaching sessions accessible and appropriate to people of all ages? List the ways in the space provided below.

. . . .

. . . .

. . . .

. . . .

. . . .

. . . .

4.5 Economically Disadvantaged People

Sports participation and access to coaching and competition are significantly lower in disadvantaged communities, but research identifies that this is a supply side problem. Provide accessible sport that meets local community need and people will come. This is called the doorstep sport approach.

Doorstep sport

As a coach, the key questions you should be asking yourself to ensure you meet the needs of disadvantaged communities are:

*   Is my session at the right time?

*   Is my session in the right place?

*   Is it delivered for the right price?

*   Most importantly, is it delivered in the right style?

Remember, you are not alone in finding the answers to these questions. Lots of statutory and voluntary organisations work in the disadvantaged communities you want to work in, and you can buddy up to do your research and get your offer right. Lots of StreetGames projects use the following people to shape the locale of their sessions: youth workers/centres, faith centres, health professionals, community police officers, housing association workers, residents' associations and existing group members.

Doorstep sport coaches

The skills and attributes of the coach are critical, and doorstep sport can be a challenging environment. You will need to be able to run exciting sessions for groups that will not necessarily warm to skills and drills. You need strong coaching skills, but also empathy and an awareness of the practical and emotional issues that may face participants.

As a doorstep sport coach, you will need to:

*   create sessions that build on the mood and interests of the group

*   build trust

*   act as a role model, mentor and motivator

*   be non-judgemental, positive and welcoming

*   signpost and support transitions to further sporting opportunities

*   adapt sessions to inferior facilities.

Encourage other coaches at your club to attend the sports coach UK 'Equity in Your Coaching' workshop. Workshop dates and locations are available from the Workshop Booking Centre.

See page 108 for contact details of the Workshop Booking Centre.

Act Appropriately

*   In order to create a positive, welcoming coaching environment, make sure you use language that is sensitive, appropriate and relevant, so as not to upset or offend people who are economically disadvantaged. It can be difficult to know what is acceptable and unacceptable – refer back to Section Three for guidance.

Seek Advice

If in doubt, contact organisations that can offer help and advice.

See pages 119–133 for contact details.

Bear in mind the information on the preceding page as you complete this activity.

ACTIVITY 7

Scenario 24

A judo club in Newham begins providing 2–3 evening sessions each week in the local community centre, which is located in the heart of a housing estate in Newham.

Although most club members were beginners when they joined, there has been significant development, with clear pathways provided. Many of the young people attending are now orange belts and take part in competitions such as the London Youth Games, National British Schools Competition and a range of local competitions. There is no need to buy expensive kit: participants can turn up and play in tracksuit, shorts and T-shirt.

The club's weekly programme has been expanded to accommodate demand, and it recently moved into a new, larger venue within Newham College, which located nearby. The club's programme now also includes a women-only session on a Wednesday evening, led by a female coach and provided as part of PlaySport, London's free sport grants programme.

British Judo has provided support to help the club develop and is currently working to encourage increased volunteer involvement by parents and local residents. The passion and drive of the head coach has played a critical part in the growth of the club. He really enjoys his coaching and has a natural ability when it comes to working with and delivering the sport to children. He has a good connection with the community and schools, and the children love taking part. To promote the club's activities, there are regular taster sessions, developing links with local groups/organisations, newsletters, schools links and liaison with local authority communication teams, as well as all-important direct engagement with key target groups in the community and word of mouth.

Stop and consider

How was the club made more accessible to people from socially and economically disadvantaged backgrounds? List the ways in the space provided below.

Feedback

- The drive and skills of the lead coach – the coaches live locally to the community and therefore have a good rapport, and are able to interact well, with participants, as well as delivering sessions that are fun, interesting and challenging.

- The club provides support to assist in the upskilling of local coaches and volunteers to help develop the local sporting infrastructure and club sustainability.

- The club uses an accessible, local, friendly and safe environment to host sessions.

- It provides clear development pathways and progression opportunities, with regular opportunities for participants to take part in appropriate competitions and gradings. This improves the participants' self-esteem and increases pride in their club and community.

- The club offers a relaxed attitude to clothing. There is no demand to buy expensive kit.

- Promotion of the club through try-out sessions and word of mouth through the community helps to strengthen the local population further, as do positive results from local and national competitions.

4.6 Lesbian, Gay, Bisexual and Transgender People

Don't Make Assumptions

- Don't assume that people attending your coaching sessions are not lesbian, gay, bisexual and transgender. It is not possible to identify someone as lesbian, gay, bisexual or transgender by the way they look or act. Think back to the barriers to participation identified in Section 2.6.

- Don't assume gay and bisexual men will not be interested in sport or that all lesbians already participate in sport. All communities consist of individuals with a range of abilities, experiences and interests.

- Don't make assumptions about the capabilities of gay men, lesbians and bisexual people and accept all participants in the gender in which they present. All participants should be assessed individually to establish their current level of ability.

Communicate

- Consult lesbian, gay, bisexual and transgender people to find out what sort of activities they are interested in. There are over 100 lesbian, gay, bisexual and transgender sports groups in the UK. You may want to contact one of these or consult with your local lesbian, gay, bisexual and transgender community organisation.

- Use language that is appropriate and does not exclude lesbians and gay men. For example, refer to people's 'partners' rather than 'husbands' or 'wives' if you don't know about the sexuality of participants (lesbians, gay men and bisexual people are unable to marry same-sex partners in the UK, but are able to create civil partnerships).

- Avoid language that undermines male participants' masculinity (eg 'don't be a wimp') as these expressions can be perceived as homophobic even if this is not your intention.

Cater for Different Needs

- Understand the barriers that may discourage lesbian, gay, bisexual and transgender people from participating in sport.

  - Many gay and bisexual men have had very negative experiences of school sport. In fact, school sport may have been an environment in which lesbian, gay, bisexual and transgender people have experienced homophobic and transphobic bullying.

  - Many lesbian, gay, bisexual and transgender people underestimate their competence in sport, and this may be expressed through statements such as 'sport just isn't for me'.

  - While it may be true that many lesbians participate in sport, it is equally true that many don't. Some lesbians may feel intimidated because they don't feel they conform to a stereotypical feminine image.

  - Transgender people may or may not feel comfortable in communal single-sex changing rooms. Attempt to provide changing rooms with cubicles where possible for all participants and always consult transgender people about what they want.

- Understand the legal requirements under which you practise. Lesbian, gay, bisexual and transgender people are protected by the Equality Act 2010:

  - Lesbian, gay, bisexual and transgender people are protected from discrimination, harassment and victimisation.

  - When transgender people participate in sport, they should be accepted in the gender role with which they present. The only exception to this can be made if there is evidence, in very limited circumstances, that the participant has an unfair advantage, or there is a risk to the safety of competitors that might occur in some close contact sports. This need not occur in most recreational and training environments, which should be made as inclusive as possible of transgender people.

Seek Advice

If in doubt, contact organisations that can offer help and advice.

See pages 119–133 for contact details.

Bear the information on the preceding page in mind as you complete the following activity.

ACTIVITY 8

Read through the following scenario. As you do, try to identify if the local authority is promoting its services to lesbian, gay, bisexual and transgender people sensitively and appropriately.

Scenario 25

The local authority has planned to promote a gay and lesbian games to improve access to sports clubs and societies for people who are lesbian, gay, bisexual and transgender. The planning group talks to national groups representing lesbian, gay, bisexual and transgender people, to ensure the event is promoted sensitively and appropriately. The planning group involves representatives of these national groups, local lesbian, gay, bisexual and transgender sports groups and also advertises for people to become members of the planning group.

The event is planned at a weekend and is linked to a broader festival. It is also organised by local people who wish to celebrate their sexuality. The event has a series of sports with 'come and try it' sessions run by local clubs who are also seeking to increase membership. The event is advertised nationally and regionally in appropriate media to attract lesbian, gay, bisexual and transgender people to the event. Locally, it is advertised on the advice of the planning group and proves a great success, with many people joining local clubs.

Stop and consider

How has the local authority increased the opportunities for people who are gay, lesbian, bisexual and transgender? List the ways in the space provided below.

4.7 Summary

This section has identified ways to make your coaching sessions more accessible and appropriate for people from the key target groups. General points that apply to all the groups are shown in the diagram on the next page.

However, despite your best efforts to ensure your coaching sessions are as equitable as possible, you cannot guarantee everyone who attends them will behave in an equitable way. Section Five provides guidance on how to challenge instances of inequitable behaviour that could arise during your coaching sessions.

COACH

DON'T MAKE ASSUMPTIONS ABOUT:

- which sports people are interested in
- which sports people are able to do
- people's reasons for taking part in sport – these are usually the same, regardless of ability, ethnic group, gender, age, background or sexuality
- people's reasons for not taking part in sport – just because you may not currently coach many people from the key target groups doesn't mean they aren't interested in your sport.

COMMUNICATE

- Consult people from the key target groups about their needs and aspirations.
- Consult organisations that can help you meet the needs of the key target groups.
- Use language that is sensitive, appropriate and relevant.
- Advertise your coaching sessions adequately, appropriately and in the right places.
- Encourage other coaches at your club to attend workshops relating to equity issues.

CATER FOR DIFFERENT NEEDS

- Understand the barriers to participation that may put people off attending your coaching sessions.
- Be aware of the needs and aspirations of people from the key target groups.
- Identify safety and medical issues.
- Hold your coaching sessions at convenient venues that are accessible and safe, with sessions at convenient times that are considerate of cultural and religious responsibilities.
- Keep the cost of your coaching sessions as low as possible. Consider subsidies with a view to providing sustainable solutions.

SEEK ADVICE

Contact organisations that can offer help and advice.

See pages 119–133 for contact details.

PARTICIPATION

5.0 What's In It For You?

As a coach, you not only have a responsibility to behave equitably yourself, but you also play an important role in promoting equitable behaviour among your participants. It is important to recognise that, despite your best efforts to be a good role model, incidents of inequitable behaviour may arise during your coaching sessions.

By the end of this section, you should be able to:

- anticipate the kind of inequitable behaviour that could arise in your coaching sessions

- select appropriate ways of dealing with it.

Challenging inequitable behaviour doesn't mean adopting the role of equity police and judging participants' behaviour. Remember, people may not be aware that the way they are behaving is unacceptable. Your role is to raise participants' awareness of sports equity issues and help them become more equitable.

5.1 Anticipating Inequitable Behaviour

Inequitable behaviour can be verbal, written or physical. Examples of each type are shown in the table below.

Type of Inequitable Behaviour	Examples
Verbal	<ul><li>Racist, sexist or homophobic language.</li><li>Ridicule or bullying because of a personal characteristic (eg wearing glasses, being disabled).</li></ul>
Written	<ul><li>All of the above written in some way (eg graffiti, in a letter, mobile phone text messages).</li></ul>
Physical	Action taken against somebody because of their race, gender, personal characteristics, sexuality. Examples include: – pushing – punching – biting – tripping somebody up and pretending it was an accident – touching somebody inappropriately – stealing or destroying other people's property – excluding somebody from taking part.

Inequitable behaviour can have a profound effect on the individual or groups of people it is directed against. This is highlighted in the example below.

Points of Interest

In November 2000, the NSPCC published the results of major research[11] carried out to explore the childhood experience of young people in the UK, including their experience of abuse and neglect. The survey found:

- 43% of the young people questioned identified bullying or being discriminated against by other children as the most common source of distress and misery
- bullying occurred mostly because of personal characteristics such as size, dress, race or manner of speech
- name calling and verbal abuse were the most common forms of bullying
- 14–15% of the young people questioned were physically attacked
- many reported having had their property stolen or damaged.

The report concludes that, for many children, the wider world of school, friends and community contains threats of bullying and discrimination and, for girls in particular, sexual harassment and violence.

Although it would be impossible to account for every eventuality, anticipating the kind of inequitable behaviour that could arise during your coaching sessions will mean you are better prepared to deal with any incidences that may occur. The next activity asks you to identify examples of inequitable behaviour from a list of coaching scenarios.

---

[11] NSPCC (2000) *Child Maltreatment in the United Kingdom: A Study of the Prevalence of Child Abuse and Neglect.* London: NSPCC.

ACTIVITY 9

Read through the following scenarios and decide which are examples of equitable and inequitable behaviour. Put a tick in the appropriate column to indicate your response. If you decide a scenario is an example of inequitable behaviour, note what type it is – verbal, written or physical.

	Scenario	Equitable	Inequitable
1	You are coaching a group of men and you hear one player telling the rest of the team they are useless and playing like a bunch of girls.		
2	You find out one of the children you coach has received a note signed by other team members, telling her she's no longer wanted on the team because she's too fat.		
3	One of the players you coach scores a good goal and is congratulated by the rest of the team		
4	You coach both men and women at your club. You notice that every time you coach two of the younger women, several of the men watch and make remarks about the way they are dressed and other suggestive comments, which the women obviously find upsetting.		
5	Other participants could be heard saying lesbians are man haters and they are trying to encourage younger players to become lesbians.		
6	A member of the team you coach has not been involved in the sport for long. Other team members are supportive and always react positively to the efforts of the new member, even if it sometimes means they lose possession of the ball.		
7	Several of your club's members are from minority ethnic communities. One day, one of these members draws your attention to a poster on the coaching noticeboard, which has been defaced with racist graffiti. You are given the name of the perpetrators, one of whom is a star player at the club.		

Scenario	Equitable	Inequitable
8 After a training session, you enter a changing room to see several young participants taunting another participant who wears glasses. One person even takes his glasses from him and stands on them.		
9 When asked to vote for the player of the year, the team you coach vote for a club member who is not the best player in the team, but is reliable, supportive and always turns up for training.		
10 You hear one of your participants telling another participant he is playing 'like a spastic'.		
11 You overhear one of your team members telling a racist joke, stating that all Muslims are terrorists.		

	Scenario	Equitable	Inequitable
1	You are coaching a group of men and you hear one player telling the rest of the team they are useless and playing like a bunch of girls.		✔ Verbal
2	You find out one of the children you coach has received a note signed by other team members, telling her she's no longer wanted on the team because she's too fat.		✔ Written
3	One of the players you coach scores a good goal and is congratulated by the rest of the team.	✔	
4	You coach both men and women at your club. You notice that every time you coach two of the younger women, several of the men watch and make remarks about the way they are dressed and other suggestive comments, which the women obviously find upsetting.		✔ Verbal
5	Other participants could be heard saying lesbians are man haters and they are trying to encourage younger players to become lesbians.		✔ Verbal
6	A member of the team you coach has not been involved in the sport for long. Other team members are supportive and always react positively to the efforts of the new member, even if it sometimes means they lose possession of the ball.	✔	

Scenario	Equitable	Inequitable
7 Several of your club's members are from minority ethnic communities. One day, one of these members draws your attention to a poster on the coaching noticeboard, which has been defaced with racist graffiti. You are given the name of the perpetrators, one of whom is a star player at the club.		✔ Written
8 After a training session, you enter a changing room to see several young participants taunting another participant who wears glasses. One person even takes his glasses from him and stands on them.		✔ Physical
9 When asked to vote for the player of the year, the team you coach vote for a club member who is not the best player in the team, but is reliable, supportive and always turns up for training.	✔	
10 You hear one of your participants telling another participant he is playing 'like a spastic'.		✔ Verbal
11 You overhear one of your team members telling a racist joke, stating that all Muslims are terrorists.		✔ Verbal

5.2 Dealing with Inequitable Behaviour

You should always challenge inequitable behaviour in a positive way. The panel below provides some useful points to bear in mind.

Points of Interest

- Having a code of practice will make it easier to deal with inequitable behaviour (eg being able to suspend or expel participants for unacceptable behaviour). Establish a code of practice that is part of the conditions of membership of your club or team. This could include things such as:

  – treating each other with respect

  – not using racist or sexist language

  – praising effort

  – not bullying or ridiculing other participants

  – acting sensitively with regard to the feelings of others.

- Avoid confrontation.

- Select the most appropriate time and place to challenge inequitable behaviour (eg discreetly during breaks or directly in front of the rest of the group).

- Act as you would want participants to act (ie be a good role model).

- Use language that is relevant, sensitive and appropriate.

- Devise a way to punish persistent offenders (eg suspend or fine players who break the code of practice).

- Devise a way to reward fair play and equitable behaviour.

- Point out that just because a team member doesn't appear to mind being referred to in an inequitable way, does not mean everyone else will put up with it.

The next activity takes the examples of inequitable behaviour from Activity 9 and asks you to think about how you would deal with them.

ACTIVITY 10

Re-read the examples of inequitable behaviour and make a note of how you would deal with them in the right-hand column. Don't worry if you find this difficult – some suggestions are provided on pages 76–78.

Scenario	How to Deal With It
1 You are coaching a group of men and you hear one player telling the rest of the team they are useless and playing like a bunch of girls.	
2 You find out one of the children you coach has received a note signed by other team members, telling her she's no longer wanted on the team because she's too fat.	
3 You coach both men and women at your club. You notice that every time you coach two of the younger women, several of the men watch and make remarks about the way they are dressed and other suggestive comments, which the women obviously find upsetting.	
4 You are told some lesbian participants who attend your coaching sessions are frequently heard telling some of the young girls at the club that men are 'no good' and they 'can't be trusted'.	

	Scenario
5 Several of your club's members are from minority ethnic communities. One day, one of these members draws your attention to a poster on the coaching noticeboard, which has been defaced with racist graffiti. You are given the name of the perpetrators, one of whom is a star player at the club.	
6 After a training session, you enter a changing room to see several young participants taunting another participant who wears glasses. One person even takes his glasses from him and stands on them.	
7 You hear one of your participants telling another participant he is playing 'like a spastic'.	
8 You overhear one of your team members telling a racist joke, stating that all Muslims are terrorists.	

Feedback

The table below contains suggested ways of dealing with the examples of inequitable behaviour in Activity 10. These are by no means the only methods – you may well have come up with others that would be more appropriate for your coaching situation.

Scenario	How to Deal With It
1 You are coaching a group of men and you hear one player telling the rest of the team they are useless and playing like a bunch of girls.	• Take the participant to one side and suggest that this is not an appropriate way to talk because it implies women are not as good at sport as men. It is also not positive to tell a group they are useless. Remind the participant of the club's code of practice. • Alternatively, talk to the whole group and ask them how they felt about being spoken to in that way and, more importantly, how they think women would have felt if they had overheard what was said.
2 You find out one of the children you coach has received a note signed by other team members, telling her she's no longer wanted on the team because she's too fat.	• Speak to the team as a whole (and their parents, if relevant) and tell them you have found out that some unfair behaviour has been going on, which has upset one team member in particular. Say how disappointed you are with their behaviour and that, unless it stops, you may have to take further action (eg cancelling a tournament or trip to see a professional game). • Speak to the child who received the note (and perhaps a parent). Make it clear you support her and try to boost her self-esteem.
3 You coach both men and women at your club. You notice that every time you coach two of the younger women, several of the men watch and make remarks about the way they are dressed and other suggestive comments, which the women obviously find upsetting.	• Speak to the men and point out they are breaking the club's code of practice and upsetting the women involved. • If the men continue to behave inequitably, you could exclude or suspend them (if this is allowed under your club constitution or code of practice).
4 You are told some lesbian participants who attend your coaching sessions are frequently heard telling some of the young girls at the club that men are 'no good' and they 'can't be trusted'.	• Talk to the women and ask them to keep their opinions to themselves. Point out that their language is sexist and not acceptable. • Remind them of the club's code of practice and ask them to try to act in a positive way by supporting the male club members.

Scenario	How to Deal With It
5 Several of your club's members are from minority ethnic communities. One day, one of these members draws your attention to a poster on the coaching noticeboard, which has been defaced with racist graffiti. You are given the name of the perpetrators, one of whom is a star player at the club.	• Establish whether or not the names you have been given are correct. • Talk to the participants involved and point out that their actions are racist and will not be tolerated at the club. You could also tell them they could be suspended or thrown out of the club because of their behaviour (if this is allowed under your club constitution or code of practice). • The fact one of the perpetrators is a star player should not affect the way you act, unless you use it to emphasise that he is a role model for other club members and should therefore act equitably. • Ask the perpetrators to post a written apology on the noticeboard and to make a verbal apology to the club members from ethnic minority communities. • If you are unable to establish who the perpetrators are, speak to the club as a whole, highlighting the club's code of practice and the action that could be taken against those who go against it. You could also put up posters reminding players of their responsibility to act in an equitable way towards each other.
6 After a training session, you enter a changing room to see several young participants taunting another participant who wears glasses. One person even takes his glasses from him and stands on them.	• Speak to the team as a whole (and, if relevant, their parents) and let them know you have found out that some inequitable behaviour has been going on, which has upset one team member in particular. • Say how disappointed you are with their behaviour and that, unless it stops, you may have to take further action (eg cancelling a tournament or trip to see a professional game). You could suspend the participant who stood on the glasses (if this is allowed under your club constitution or code of practice). • Speak to the participant who was on the receiving end of the taunts (and his parents, if relevant). Make it clear you support him and try to boost his self-esteem.

7 You hear one of your participants telling another participant he is playing 'like a spastic'.	• Speak to the participant individually.
	
	• Point out that his language is unacceptable because it:
	  – is wrong to refer to a person with cerebral palsy as a spastic
	  – implies that somebody with a disability is less capable of taking part in sport than somebody without.
	
	• Remind him of the club's code of practice.

Scenario	How to Deal With It
8 You overhear one of your team members telling a racist joke, stating that all Muslims are terrorists.	• Talk to the participants involved, including the joke teller and audience. Point out that their actions are racist and oppressive, and that they will not be tolerated at the club .You could also tell them they could be suspended or thrown out of the club because of their behaviour (if this is allowed under your club constitution or code of practice). • Explain the inaccuracies of their joke and also explain that prejudice and stereotypes are often based on misinformation.

5.3 Summary

You should now feel more comfortable about dealing with inequitable behaviour. Remember, this doesn't mean adopting the role of equity police and judging participants' behaviour, but raising awareness of equity issues and helping participants become more equitable. Doing so will help create a safe and enjoyable sporting environment for everyone.

Try to set a good example and promote good practice at all times. Doing so not only encourages your participants to behave appropriately, it also ensures the way you coach is equitable and protects you from allegations that could otherwise be made against you. Failure to act in an equitable way not only constitutes poor coaching practice, in some instances, it may even be against the law. Section Six looks at the sources of liability that may affect coaches.

6.0 What's In It For You?

As described in Section One, providing sporting opportunities for everyone in society is not just a moral responsibility, but could also be a legal requirement in some instances, particularly for organisations deemed to be service providers (eg local authorities, governing bodies of sport, sporting organisations).

The Equality Act 2010

Outgoing discrimination laws had helped make progress on equality, but because they had been developed over more than 40 years, they had become complex and difficult for people to understand and navigate. The Equality Act 2010 was implemented fully from 6 April 2011 and served to streamline and consolidate much of the existing equity law, including:

*   the Equal Pay Act 1970

*   the Sex Discrimination Act 1975

*   the Race Relations Act 1976

*   the Disability Discrimination Act 1995.

The Act brings together for the first time all the legal requirements on equality that the private, public and voluntary sectors need to follow. It affects equality law at work and in delivering all sorts of services and running clubs.

The Equality Act and running a club, society or association

If you run a club, society or association, the Equality Act helps you to understand how best to deal with a range of potential membership issues. In general, you should not:

*   treat an existing or potential member, guest or associate worse than someone else because of a protected characteristic

*   refuse membership or grant membership on less favourable terms because of their protected characteristics.

You can restrict membership on some grounds, for example to people who share a protected characteristic where the main purpose of the club is to bring people together who share that characteristic (eg a health support club for gay people).

You don't have to make reasonable adjustments where these would fundamentally alter the club's purpose (eg if a competitive swimming club is asked to adjust their pool water temperature to accommodate swimmers with a disability).

Associations and the people who run them must not harass or victimise members, those seeking to be members or associate members or guests and those seeking to be guests.

6.1 Definitions

The following definitions exist within the Equality Act. Examples have been provided in some cases to clarify the definitions.

Discrimination

This includes:

*   treating a person worse than someone else because of a protected characteristic (known as **direct discrimination**), although in the case of pregnancy and maternity direct discrimination, this can occur if they have a protected characteristic without needing to compare treatment to someone else

*   putting in place a rule or way of doing things that has a worse impact on someone with a protected characteristic than someone without one, when this cannot be objectively justified (known as **indirect discrimination**)

*   treating a disabled person unfavourably because of something connected with their disability when this cannot be justified (known as discrimination arising from disability)

*   failing to make reasonable adjustments for disabled people.

Discrimination by association

- Definition: this is direct discrimination against someone because they associate with another person who possesses a protected characteristic.

- For example, June works as a project manager and is looking forward to a promised promotion. However, after she tells her boss that her mother, who lives at home, has had a stroke, the promotion is withdrawn as the boss thinks June will not have time to concentrate on her job due to caring responsibilities for her mother.

- This may be discrimination because of June's **association** with a disabled person.

Discrimination by perception

- Definition: this is direct discrimination against an individual because others think they possess a particular protected characteristic. It applies even if the person does not possess that characteristic.

- For example, Mary is 45 but looks much younger. Many people assume she is in her mid-20s. She is not allowed to represent her company at an international meeting because the managing director thinks she is too young.

- Mary has been discriminated against on the perception of a protected characteristic.

Combined discrimination

- Definition: when a person is discriminated against because of a combination of two relevant protected characteristics.

- For example, Julie is a 55-year-old newsreader who is dismissed and replaced with a 30-year-old female newsreader. The age of male newsreaders, employed at the same network, ranges from 31–58. It clearly wasn't Julie's sex alone that led to the decision to let her go since she was replaced by a female. It presumably also wasn't a question of her age as a fellow newsreader was 58. This was potentially a case of an individual being discriminated against due to a combination of characteristics.

Harassment

Unwanted conduct that has the purpose or effect of violating someone's dignity or that is hostile, degrading, humiliating or offensive to someone with a protected characteristic or in a way that is sexual in nature.

Victimisation

Treating someone unfavourably because they have taken (or might be taking) action under the Equality Act or supporting somebody who is doing so.

As well as these characteristics, the law also protects people from being discriminated against:

- by someone who wrongly perceives them to have one of the protected characteristics

- because they are associated with someone who has a protected characteristic – this includes the parent of a disabled child or adult or someone else who is caring for a disabled person.

Whether you are an employed or voluntary coach, it is important you are aware of the legal framework that affects equity.

Positive Action or Positive Discrimination

Positive action refers to a variety of measures designed to counteract the effects of past discrimination and to help eliminate stereotyping.

Positive action is lawful and, as such, requires an evidence base to justify your actions. This could include gaps identified by research, audits or monitoring data. For example, the provision of Muslim women-only coaching sessions if evidence shows this particular target group is under-represented.

Positive discrimination, however, is unlawful (unless a genuine occupational requirement applies to a particular post) and involves treating people more favourably just because they are from an under-represented group, or less favourably because they are from an over-represented group. For instance, appointing a person purely on the grounds of his/her race or gender, rather than on that person's ability to do the job in question.

UK Sport Equalities Legislation – A Guide for Governing Bodies of Sport. Adapted and reproduced by kind permission of UK Sport and the Sports Councils Equity Group.

Legislation, as identified in Section One, is in place to make sure people are not discriminated against in the workplace and while accessing services. The aim of this section is to provide some detail and help you understand how these key pieces of legislation could affect your coaching practice.

Liability

Employers can be held accountable for the action of their employees in the first instance. This means that, even if an employer would not encourage or sanction acts of discrimination, it is still liable for any discriminatory acts committed by its employees.

Employers have a legal defence available to them, which is that they have taken such steps as were reasonably practicable to prevent the employee from committing a discriminatory act.

6.2 Legislation

Let's take a look at some of the legislation in more detail:

Equal Pay

Equal pay legislation requires equal treatment for women (and men) in pay and other contractual conditions of service. A woman only has to show she is doing like, equivalent or equal value of work to a man.

Women and men are entitled to equal pay and conditions if:

- they are employed on like work, which means their work is the same or broadly similar

- their jobs have been given equivalent rating under a non-discriminatory job evaluation scheme

- their work is of equal value, in terms of effort, skill, decision making or other demands.

In many instances, males and females do not receive the same rates of pay for comparable work, despite the age of this legislation.

Implications For You

Your rate of pay should match that of other coaches qualified to the same level and with the same degree of experience in your sport.

Sex Discrimination

Sex discrimination legislation means it is unlawful to discriminate directly or indirectly on the grounds of a person's sex and marital status, including gender reassignment. It is unlawful for employers to discriminate in recruitment, promotion, training and transfer, terms and conditions of employment, and dismissal. Legislation also protects transgender people from discrimination in the provision of goods and services.

Sexual harassment is a form of sexual discrimination. It is unwanted, often sexual, attention and may include:

- written or verbal abuse or threats
- sexually oriented comments
- jokes, lewd comments or sexual innuendos
- taunts about body, dress, marital status or sexuality
- shouting and/or bullying
- ridiculing or undermining of performance or self-respect
- sexual or homophobic graffiti
- practical jokes based on sex
- intimidating sexual remarks, invitations or familiarity
- domination of meetings, training sessions or equipment
- condescending or patronising behaviour
- physical contact, fondling, pinching or kissing
- sex-related vandalism
- offensive telephone calls or photos
- bullying on the basis of sex.

Text reproduced with the kind permission of WomenSport International from their leaflet *Sexual Harassment and Abuse of Girls and Women in Sport.*

In order to promote best practice when working with mixed-gender groups, you should:

- always assess participants on the basis of their ability, not gender
- have an open mind and no preconceived ideas about women's and girls' abilities, and always treat everyone fairly
- try to develop team-selection criteria based on ability, and always be able to provide written comments to justify your decision to select particular participants
- try to involve team captains or others when selecting teams, to avoid any biased decisions
- use language that is sensitive, appropriate and relevant
- ensure appropriate facilities are available to accommodate all participants' needs.

These are just some of the things to bear in mind when coaching women and girls – refer back to Section Four for further guidance.

The following organisations can offer further advice and support on working with women and girls:

- EHRC
- Equality Commission for Northern Ireland
- Women's Sport and Fitness Foundation (WSFF).

See pages 132, 133 and 127 for contact details.

Race Relations

This legislation makes it unlawful to discriminate directly or indirectly on the grounds of a person's colour, race, nationality, ethnic or national origin. It is unlawful for employers to discriminate in recruitment, promotion, training and transfer, terms and conditions of employment, and dismissal.

It gives anyone who thinks they may have been discriminated against on racial grounds (ie because of their race, colour, nationality, or ethnic or national origin) the right to seek justice in the courts or an employment tribunal. It covers the following areas:

- education
- employment
- housing
- provision of goods, facilities and services
- training.

The Act deals with people's discriminatory actions and the effect of their actions. Motives do not matter, but if someone's attitude is proven to be racist, as well as their actions being discriminatory, this will count against them in any court or tribunal.

It also makes it unlawful for any public authority, in relation to any of its activities, to discriminate on racial grounds whether directly, indirectly or by victimisation[12]. This applies not only to statutory bodies (eg local authorities), but also to any private or voluntary body when carrying out public functions.

Racist abuse and harassment (eg insensitive language, persistent remarks) are forms of racial discrimination.

Points of Interest

Incidents in public places, such as racial abuse in the street or at a football match, are not covered by the Equality Act. These are dealt with under the Public Order Act and the Football Offences Act respectively.

Race Relations (Northern Ireland) Order 1997

As advised at the begining of this resource, Northern Ireland is yet to adopt the Equality Act so the existing equality legislation that was subsumed into the Equality Act remains in force. The Race Relations (Northern Ireland) Order is based on the Race Relations Act 1976 and became law in 1997. Section 21 of the Order makes it unlawful for people who provide goods, facilities or services to the public, or a section of the public, to discriminate on racial grounds against people seeking to obtain or use those goods, facilities or services by:

- refusing or deliberately omitting to provide them with goods, facilities or services

or

- refusing or deliberately omitting to provide them with goods, facilities or services of the same quality, in the same manner and on the same terms as other members of the public.

Section 38 of the Order relates specifically to sports and competitions. It outlines circumstances when discrimination on the basis of nationality or place of birth, or the length of time somebody has been resident in a particular area or place, is acceptable.

This is only when:

- selecting one or more persons to represent a country, place or area, or any related association, in any sport or game

or

- abiding by the rules of any competition so far as they relate to eligibility to compete in any sport or game.

For further information on the Race Relations (Northern Ireland) Order 1997 and related issues, contact the Equality Commission for Northern Ireland (see page 133 for contact details).

Implications For You

At present in the UK, there are very few examples of legal proceedings that have been brought against coaches under the Race Relations Act 1976 or Race Relations (Northern Ireland) Order 1997. However, this is not to say that it couldn't happen. The paragraphs below show examples of action taken against racial discrimination in rugby league and football.

[12] See the racial discrimination entry in Appendix A for definitions of these terms.

Rugby League

In October 2000, under the outgoing Race Relations Act, an employment tribunal found Super League club Leeds Rhinos guilty of 'unconscious racial discrimination'. It ruled a black player was discriminated against when the head coach told him he would not get a first-team place 'irrespective of performance'. The head coach's comments were deemed 'ill-considered' and the club was accused of failing to adequately investigate the allegations of racial discrimination made by the player against the head coach.

Football

Although not as widespread as it was during the 1970s and 1980s, the problem of racism in football still exists. To help combat this, football authorities have begun to fine individual clubs for racial abuse committed by their fans towards opposition players from minority ethnic communities (eg UEFA fined Red Star Belgrade £16,000 for the racist behaviour of its fans towards black players in the Leicester City team during a UEFA Cup match in 2000). Rather than bringing charges of racial discrimination against individuals, football clubs are now held responsible for the behaviour of their fans.

In 2000, The FA introduced a new set of disciplinary guidelines designed to clean up the image of English football. Within these, it specifies that clubs are responsible for crowd control and face fines or points deductions if fans behave in an unacceptable manner. In addition, any offence motivated by discrimination on racial grounds will result in double the usual penalty.

In order to promote best practice when working with participants from minority ethnic communities, you should:

- always assess participants on the basis of their ability, not race

- have an open mind and no preconceived ideas about people from minority ethnic communities, and always treat everyone fairly

- always use language that is sensitive, appropriate and relevant

- ensure all participants behave appropriately during your coaching sessions and do not offend others.

These are just some of the things to bear in mind when coaching people from minority ethnic communities – refer back to Section Four for further guidance.

The following organisations can offer further advice and support on working with people from minority ethnic communities:

- EHRC

- Equality Commission for Northern Ireland

- Sporting Equals.

See pages 132, 133 and 127 for contact details.

Disability Discrimination

It is unlawful for an association with 25 or more members to discriminate against current or prospective members.

Discrimination occurs when an employee or job applicant receives less favourable treatment or is denied equal opportunities because she is disabled, and the treatment cannot be justified.

It is unlawful for a provider of goods, services or facilities to discriminate against a disabled person in:

- refusing to provide or deliberately not providing goods, services or facilities that are normally provided to members of the public

- offering a lower standard of goods, services and facilities

- terms of the goods, services and facilities provided.

In practice, this means that service providers cannot discriminate against a disabled person by:

- refusing to provide a service

- offering a worse standard of service

- offering a service on worse terms

- failing to comply with their duty to make reasonable adjustments.

Service providers must treat disabled people in the same way they would treat other people when offering a service or facility, whether for payment or not. In addition, they must make all reasonable adjustments to the environment in which they operate, to accommodate an individual's impairment.

This involves:

- changing any policies, practices and procedures that might discriminate against disabled people

- providing auxiliary aids and services

- providing their services by a reasonable alternative means, if there is a physical barrier to access

- making sure that private clubs with 25 or more members cannot keep disabled people out, just because they have a disability.

Sports clubs have to make reasonable adjustments for disabled people, such as providing extra help, or making changes to the way they provide their services. This also covers the physical features of their premises, to overcome physical barriers to access.

Implications For You

In order to promote best practice when deciding whether to involve disabled people in your coaching sessions, you should:

- always assess participants on the basis of their ability, not disability

- have an open mind and no preconceived ideas about what level of performance you think a particular participant is capable of

- advertise your coaching sessions in the right places

- find out if your governing body of sport has any recommendations on how to involve disabled people in your coaching sessions

- establish whether you would need specialist equipment

- find out about workshops/courses you could attend to improve your knowledge of coaching disabled people.

Some past court cases relating to disability discrimination include:

Golf

Vernon Roper, who has multiple sclerosis, was refused permission by his local golf club to use a motorised golf cart, apparently on the basis that to do so would lead to irreparable damage to the turf. In particular, it was suggested by the golf club that the turf had only recently been laid and that, until it had a chance to settle, there was no prospect of the client being allowed to use a motorised cart.

The court decided the golf course unlawfully discriminated against the claimant by failing to discharge its legal duty to make an adjustment to allow the client to make use of its services. A reasonable adjustment was for the defendant to allow the claimant to use his golf cart on the course in dry weather conditions. Health and safety concerns did not make the adjustment requested unreasonable, nor did they justify the failure to make the reasonable adjustment.

Rugby Union

The client, who is a wheelchair user, alleged unfavourable treatment by a rugby ground in its provisions for disabled fans. Rugby union rules state that a disabled person must be accompanied by a non-disabled person. This rule means the client must purchase two tickets for each game he wishes to attend, although the one for his companion is at a reduced rate. In addition, although the client joined the rugby union's disabled fans' register, he was not offered seating on the terrace, since the union's rule was that this was prioritised for those who had a disability as a result of playing rugby.

The rugby ground owners have agreed to change almost all of their ticketing policies and redesign their various forms. They are developing new policies, which they will agree with the EHRC as part of a final settlement. They have also agreed to train all staff in disability equality.

sports coach UK Workshops

* How to Coach Disabled People in Sport
* Inclusive Coaching: Disability.

Workshop dates and locations are available from the Workshop Booking Centre.

See page 108 for contact details of the Workshop Booking Centre.

Governing Body of Sport Courses

Many governing bodies of sport run courses designed to assist those working with disabled sportspeople. Find out what your governing body of sport has to offer.

These are just some of the things to bear in mind when coaching disabled people – refer back to Section Four for further guidance.

The following organisations can offer further advice and support on working with disabled people:

* Disability Sport Wales
* Disability Sports NI (DSNI)
* EFDS
* local disability rights organisation (if one is available)
* local authority
* Royal National Institute for Blind People (RNIB) and for Deaf People (RNID)
* Scottish Disability Sport
* EHRC.

See pages 123–125 and 132 for contact details.

Sexual Orientation

Sexual orientation discrimination occurs when someone is treated less favourably because of their sexual orientation, their perceived sexual orientation, or the sexual orientation of those with whom they associate.

Religion and Belief

Employers are advised to make adjustments to ensure employees are not prevented from expressing their religion or belief while at work. Adjustments may include allowing time and space to pray, and not holding major meetings or events during religious festivals.

These regulations outlaw discrimination in employment and vocational training on the grounds of sexual orientation, religion and belief. They also outlaw direct and indirect discrimination, harassment and victimisation.

Other Existing Legislation that may be of Interest to You

Employment Rights Act 1996

This Act gives parents the right to request flexible working arrangements.

Rehabilitation of Offenders Act 1974

This Act enables some criminal convictions to become spent or ignored after a rehabilitation period. A rehabilitation period is a set length of time from the date of conviction. After this period, with certain exceptions, an ex-offender is not normally obliged to mention the conviction when applying for a job or insurance. Exceptions to the Act, where people will be expected to declare convictions even if they are spent, include appointment to any post providing care/schooling/training/supervision to people under the age of 18, or vulnerable adults. Criminal record checks will reveal both spent and unspent convictions.

Employment Protection (Consolidation) Act 1978

This Act provides the statutory maternity rights scheme. Under this provision, employers are required to make statutory maternity payments to women employees who have to go on maternity leave.

These rights allow the woman employee to return to the same job or suitable alternative work after the maternity period. The Act ensures women on maternity leave cannot be made redundant.

Children Act 1989 and 2004

This Act has reformed the law relating to children and has brought together public and private law about children.

General Duty of the EHRC

The Commission shall exercise its functions under Part II of the Equality Act 2006 with a view to encouraging and supporting the development of a society in which:

- people's ability to achieve their potential is not limited by prejudice or discrimination

- there is respect for, and protection of, each individual's human rights

- there is respect for the dignity and worth of each individual

- each individual has an equal opportunity to participate in society

- there is mutual respect between groups, based on understanding and valuing diversity, and on shared respect for equality and human rights.

Points of Interest

Code of Practice for Sports Coaches

sports coach UK has developed a *Code of Practice for Sports Coaches* in order to establish, publicise and maintain standards of ethical behaviour in coaching practice, and to inform and protect members of the public using the services of sports coaches. The Code forms the Values Statement underpinning the National Occupational Standards for Coaching, Teaching and Instructing, reviewed in 2004, led by SkillsActive.

The Code states:

Coaches must respect the rights, dignity and worth of every human being and their ultimate right to self-determination. Specifically, coaches must treat everyone equitably and sensitively, within the context of their activity and ability, regardless of gender, ethnic origin, cultural background, sexual orientation, religion or political affiliation.

sports coach UK Code of Practice for Sports Coaches (2005)

The status of the coach continues to increase in the perception of the public at large, so it is therefore crucial for you to adopt and abide by the Code, which reflects the highest standards of good coaching practice. In doing so, you accept your responsibility to:

- sports participants and their parents/families

- coaching and other colleagues

- your governing body

- your coaching employer

- society.

To obtain a copy of the Code, contact 1st4sport.com (see page 108 for contact details).
For further information about sports coach UK membership services, contact 0113-290 7612.

What Are the Public Sector Equality Duties?

The first of the Equality Duties (race) was introduced in 2002 following The Macpherson Report and its conclusion that some organisations were institutionally racist. The public sector duties (now including gender and disability) are a positive and proactive means to bring about much wider cultural change within society, with the aim of improving the treatment of employees and better delivering public services for all.

Duties will be extended to cover religion or belief, sexual orientation and age, under proposals for a Single Equality Act, estimated to be in place in 2010.

What Do the Equality Duties Involve?

Each of the three sets of Equality Duties has two main elements – the 'General Duty' and the 'Specific Duties'.

The dual aims at the heart of the General Duty are the:

- promotion of equality of opportunity for all
- elimination of discrimination and harassment.

These basic principles are expanded uniquely for each of the protected characteristics involved.

The Specific Duties give a framework to help organisations achieve the General Duty. The main focus of the Specific Duties under each of the eight protected characteristics is the preparation, publication and implementation of an Equality Scheme (in essence an action plan), which should demonstrate how an organisation intends to fulfil its obligations.

How Are Governing Bodies and Coaches Affected By the Equality Duties?

Both the General and Specific aspects of all three sets of Equality Duties explicitly apply to certain public authorities, which, in all likelihood, provide funding for your organisation and with whom you work in partnership. These include all sports councils; the Department for Culture, Media and Sport (DCMS); and local authorities.

In order for these public authorities to implement their Duties fully, the following types of demands may exist:

- Your continued funding may be attached to certain conditions, such as achievement of specific levels of the Equality/Equity Standard: A Framework for Sport.

- Your policies will need to be compliant with current legislation.

- You will need to monitor the number of participants, members, coaches, officials, spectators and volunteers, with reference to each of the protected characteristics.

- Targets will need to be set for increased participation among under-represented groups.

In cases where a governing body is performing 'functions of a public nature', you will be directly affected as you will be expected to comply with the General Duty.

When considering the issue of functions of a public nature, you will need to ask the following questions of your organisation:

- Do we receive public funding?
- Do we provide a public service?
- Do we work in partnership with those public authorities explicitly covered by the Equality Duties?
- Is there a public interest in the functions of our governing body being performed?
- Is our main motivation in serving the public interest rather than profit?

If you are more likely to answer yes to these questions, then your organisation is performing functions of a public nature.

Adapted from the UK Sport Equalities Legislation – A Guide for Governing Bodies of Sport. Adapted and reproduced by kind permission of UK Sport and the Sports Councils Equity Group.

Sexual Orientation

The Act covers the provision of goods and services. The law protects those people who identify themselves as lesbian, gay, bisexual or heterosexual.

Implications For You

In the employment and, indeed, deployment of coaches, organisations should be mindful not to contravene current employment regulations.

Points of Interest

Did You Know...?

Disability

1 The Equality Act 2010 covers people:
   - with physical impairments
   - with learning disabilities
   - whose mental health is impaired
   - who use hearing aids

   ...but not people who wear glasses.

2 It is lawful to provide separate coaching sessions for disabled people, but unlawful to provide separate sessions for non-disabled people.

3 All sports facilities are legally required to provide auxiliary aids to enable disabled people to use them. Since 2004, they have also been legally required to make their premises accessible to disabled people.

Race, religion or belief

1 When selecting a team, or rules relating to eligibility to compete in a sport or game, it is sometimes lawful to discriminate on the basis of:
   - nationality
   - place of birth
   - length of time lived in a particular area

   ...but unlawful to discriminate on the basis of:

   - race or ethnic origin
   - colour.

2 It is lawful to discriminate in the provision of separate training courses for sports staff (eg training for black people in leisure management).

3 It is unlawful for ethnic groups to set up their own sporting organisations and exclude people on the grounds of ethnic origin or national group.

Gender (women and girls)

1 In some circumstances, it is lawful to provide and advertise single-gender sports facilities.

2 In some circumstances, it is unlawful to staff a women-only sports session with a male coach.

Based on information from Nottingham University (1999) 'Equality in Sport Means Quality Sport'. National Sports Development Seminar Facilitator's Pack.

6.3 Negligence

By far the most serious of the sources of liability explored in this resource would be a claim that a participant under your supervision had suffered injury, loss or damage because of your negligence as a coach. This section highlights the need for you to be aware of action that may be required of you during coaching sessions, to avoid instances of injury, loss or damage occurring, particularly when coaching disabled people.

There are four elements that, together, constitute a case for negligence:

- There exists a duty of care towards the participant.

- This duty of care imposes a standard, and negligence has caused that standard to be breached.

- The participant has suffered loss, harm, damage or injury.

- The breach of duty of care contributes to the loss, harm, damage or injury.

Points of Interest

Duty of Care

Safe

- In any coaching environment, where there is a foreseeable risk of harm (this includes indoors, outdoors, and in the wet and the dry), you must carry out a risk assessment of the activity to be performed within that environment, and be able to provide documentary evidence to support that assessment.

- No-one can completely eliminate the risk of harm, but you must show evidence of having acted reasonably to minimise risks as far as humanly possible (eg safety of venue, equipment and playing surfaces).

- Make your participants fully aware of the risks involved in particular activities. This needs to be done repeatedly, clearly and thoroughly. Remember that a novice may not necessarily have the same comprehension or appreciation of the risks as an intermediate or expert participant.

- It is important to plan and deliver appropriate coaching sessions to meet the needs of your participants. This means selecting appropriate activities for the age, physical and emotional maturity, experience, and ability of participants.

- Ensure participants are made aware of the health and safety guidelines that operate in your sport environment and within your governing body of sport.

- Reinforce and, if possible, practise emergency procedures.

- Encourage fair play and penalise incidences of foul play in your sport.

- Ensure participants stick to the rules and take as few risks as possible on their way to achieving their goals.

Qualified

- To ensure your coaching is in line with the recommended good practice advocated by your governing body of sport and sports coach UK, you should obtain coaching qualifications. Governing bodies of sport can provide sport-specific training, while sports coach UK workshops and resources[13] provide general support and guidance that underpin coach education courses.

- Your coaching qualifications should be:

  - relevant

  - at the appropriate level

  - current and up to date.

---

[13] Further details are available from sports coach UK and 1st4sport.com (see page 108 for contact details).

Competent

- You should only coach those elements of your sport for which your training and competence are recognised by your governing body of sport.

- The National Occupational Standards for Coaching, Teaching and Instructing (and/or approved governing body of sport coaching awards) provide the framework for assessing competence at the different levels of coaching practice. Competence to coach should normally be verified through evidence of qualifications. Competence cannot be inferred solely from evidence of prior experience.

- You must be able to recognise and accept when to refer participants to other coaches or agencies. It is your responsibility, as far as possible, to verify the competence and integrity of any other person to whom you refer a participant.

- You should regularly seek ways of increasing your personal and professional development.

- You should welcome evaluation of your work by colleagues and be able to account for what you do and why to participants, employers, governing bodies of sport and colleagues.

- You have a responsibility to yourself and your participants to maintain your own effectiveness, resilience and abilities. You should recognise when your personal resources are so depleted that help is needed. This may necessitate your withdrawal from coaching temporarily or permanently.

Insured

- Insurance is essential for coaches, participants and sports providers (eg coaches, local authorities, governing bodies of sport).

- Some governing bodies of sport do not allow coaches or participants to take part in their sport without insurance cover, while others include insurance as part of their affiliation fee. Check if your governing body of sport operates an insurance scheme.

- sports coach UK Membership Services provides qualified coaches with insurance as part of its benefits package.

- Insurance should cover both public liability and personal accidents, and must be adequate for the risks faced in the particular sport.

Further information on the responsibilities of coaches is available in the:

- sports coach UK *Code of Practice for Sports Coaches*[14]

- National Occupational Standards for Coaching, Teaching and Instructing[15] – Section 7.3: Values Statement and Code of Ethics for Coaching, Teaching and Instructing.

[14] Available from 1st4sport.com (see page 108 for contact details).

[15] Available from SkillsActive.

Negligence can be attributed both to your actions and your omissions. Injured participants have the right to sue coaches who may have caused injury by negligence. To do so, they would have to prove it was a breach of the standards demanded by the coach's duty of care that caused loss or injury. This is described as the 'but for' test:

But for the actions of the coach, would the loss or injury have occurred?

The following case study is an example of a court case brought by a disabled archer. It illustrates the duty of care you owe your participants.

Morrell v Owen and Others

In 1993, Mr Justice Mitchell adjudged organisers and coaches of sporting activities owe a greater duty of care to disabled people than they would to non-disabled people.

The incident that brought about this judgment occurred during a training session held in 1993 by the British Amputee and Les Autres Sports Association (BALASA) in a sports hall in Birmingham. Two activities – archery and discus – were in progress in the same sports hall, which was divided by a fishnet curtain.

Miss Morrell, a disabled archer, was injured by a discus that struck the dividing curtain and hit her on the side of the head. The coaches present claimed they had warned Miss Morrell of the dangers of the activity at the other side of the curtain. Miss Morrell, however, claimed she had not been warned. Mr Justice Mitchell believed Miss Morrell, stating the kind of misthrow that occurred was entirely foreseeable, as was the accident in question. He stated the coaches present owed a greater duty of care to disabled people than they would to non-disabled people.

Implications For You

The Morrell v Owen and Others case illustrates how important it is for you to ensure that, when coaching disabled people, you take all the necessary measures to ensure your sessions are as safe as possible. You are strongly recommended to attend workshops/courses to improve your knowledge of coaching disabled people.

sports coach UK Workshops

- How to Coach Disabled People in Sport (Coaching Essentials Workshop)

- Coaching Disabled Performers (Develop Your Coaching Workshop)

Workshop dates and locations are available from the Workshop Booking Centre.

See page 108 for contact details of the Workshop Booking Centre.

Governing Body of Sport Courses

Many governing bodies of sport run courses designed to assist those working with disabled sportspeople. Find out what your governing body of sport has to offer.

6.4 Defamation

Defamation is a statement that injures the reputation of another by exposing her to hatred, contempt or ridicule, or that tends to lower her in the esteem of right-thinking members of society.

There are two types of defamation:

- slander – the spoken word

- libel – the written word.

The following story illustrates defamation and describes a situation that could occur in any sports club at any level.

Scenario 26

Alison is a coach at a local athletics club. She successfully applies to become part of the coaching team responsible for the elite squad at the club. Tushar is an up-and-coming member of the elite squad with potential to do well at the next regional athletics meeting. He is one of five athletes Alison has specific responsibility for. However, Tushar finds it difficult to get on with Alison. She is always making derogatory remarks about him and purposefully ignores him during group coaching sessions, devoting more time to the other athletes. Tushar's performance consequently suffers and he misses out on a place in the club team.

Disappointed, Tushar asks to be moved to a different group with a different coach. Alison says Tushar's poor form has nothing to do with her and he should be more committed to his training if he wants to do well.

Tushar moves to a different group and is much happier. His performance improves dramatically and he comfortably wins the 100m final at the next regional athletics meeting. After the race, Alison is overheard telling her group of athletes Tushar is selfish and attention seeking. She adds that she doesn't know how Tushar managed to do so well and that he must have taken performance-enhancing drugs to have made such a dramatic improvement in such a short space of time.

In the example above, Alison acted in an inappropriate and unprofessional manner, and could well have lost her position as coach at the athletics club. Make sure you never put yourself in a position where this could happen to you. Always set an example to your participants, in terms of behaviour and attitude. Your professional relationship with, and attitude towards, officials, spectators and other coaches must also be of the highest standard. Think about the influence your behaviour will have on your participants, their parents and other coaches. Try to be consistent and fair in what you say, what you do and what you ask of others.

6.5 Summary

This section should have helped you understand the legal framework that affects equity. The key points you need to remember are listed over the next two pages.

DISCRIMINATION

- Discrimination is the action people take on the basis of their prejudices. It occurs when a prejudiced person has the power to put their prejudices into action, which results in unfair and unjust treatment. There are two types of discrimination – direct and indirect.

- To avoid allegations of discrimination being made against you or your employer, always promote best practice when working with people from the protected characteristics.

NEGLIGENCE

- All coaches have a duty to be:

  - safe

  - qualified

  - competent

  - insured.

  This is known as duty of care.

- Negligence on the part of the coach causes a breach of duty and can result in a participant suffering injury, loss or damage.

- To avoid allegations of negligence being made against you, ensure you are aware of action that may be required of you during coaching sessions, particularly when coaching disabled people. Remember, negligence can be attributed both to your actions and your omissions.

DEFAMATION

- Defamation is a statement that injures the reputation of another by exposing him to hatred, contempt or ridicule, or that tends to lower him in the esteem of right-thinking members of society.

- There are two types of defamation:

  - slander – the spoken word

  - libel – the written word.

- To avoid allegations of defamation being made against you, always set an example to your participants, in terms of behaviour and attitude.

7.0 What's In It For You?

By now, you should appreciate just how vital it is to ensure your coaching practice is as equitable as possible. However inspired you may feel to make improvements in the necessary areas, putting the theory into practice may seem challenging. Where do you start? To what extent should you aim to attract people from the protected characteristics to your coaching sessions?

By the end of this section, you should be able to:

- identify areas you feel need improving or developing in your coaching practice

- explain why developing an equity policy is a good idea

- develop an action plan for adopting equity principles into your coaching practice.

7.1 Identifying Areas for Change

Before you can plan for change, you need to identify the areas you feel need improving or developing. The following ideas should help you do this:

- Use the most appropriate national, regional and local population statistics as a general guide to gauge how equitable your coaching sessions are.

  See Section 1 (pages 5–9) for further details.

- Ask another coach to observe one of your coaching sessions with particular reference to equity issues (eg the language you use). Compare their feedback with your own analysis of your coaching practice.

- Talk to your participants and find out whether anything you have said or done made them feel uncomfortable (you should already be doing this anyway as part of your session evaluations). Alternatively, you could devise a questionnaire for participants to fill in anonymously in their own time.

- Find out if your governing body of sport has an equity policy. If so, get hold of a copy and make sure you follow its recommendations.

  See Section 7.2 for further details about equity policies.

- Attend sports coach UK's 'Equity in Your Coaching' workshop and/or appropriate governing body of sport courses/workshops (see Appendix B for further details).

- Contact the organisations listed in Appendix B for help and advice.

7.2 Equity Statement and Policy

Assessing how equitable your coaching sessions currently are is the first step towards ensuring they are accessible to everyone. It provides you with a starting point from which to measure your future achievements. The next stage is to demonstrate your commitment to equity.

sports coach UK has demonstrated its commitment by developing the following statement of intent:

sports coach UK is committed to the principles and practices of equal opportunities, both as an employer and in the delivery of services. Employment opportunities, programmes, products and services are available to all sections of the community and sports coach UK will not discriminate on grounds including, but not limited by, gender, race, disability, age, religious or political belief, sexual orientation, social background, ethnic origin, language, pregnancy, or marital or civil partnership status.

sports coach UK Equal Opportunities
Statement of Intent
(taken from sports coach UK's Equity Policy)

Developing a similar equity statement for your club is a good way of raising awareness, both internally and externally, of your club's commitment to providing better sporting opportunities for the key target groups. It will also help you to:

- encourage more people to participate in your sport

- encourage more people into coaching, officiating and administrating in your sport

- improve your club's public image

- show your club is responding to equity legislation and other equity-related initiatives.

As well as developing a general equity policy, you might want to create individual policies for each of the protected characteristics. For example, sports coach UK has developed a racial equality policy.

For an equity policy to work, everybody involved in your club (eg participants, coaches, employees, volunteers) needs to recognise their own practice is perhaps not as equitable as it should be, and be prepared to do something about it. There also needs to be a commitment to implementing, monitoring and evaluating the policy, which may have implications for funding for new resources, equipment and training.

You may not personally be in a position to implement an equity policy – perhaps this would be the responsibility of club management or perhaps you are self-employed and coach at a variety of different venues. However, you still have a role to play in influencing the powers that be, as well as raising the awareness of participants, colleagues and other related groups about the importance of equity. There is also nothing to stop you developing your own personal equity policy to guide your coaching practice.

7.3 Putting Theory Into Practice

This resource may have highlighted specific areas in your own coaching practice you would like to improve or change altogether. Some things will be relatively easy to improve/change (eg being aware of the words and phrases you use). Other things may take a little longer, and you may need to contact various organisations for assistance and advice. The next activity will help you focus on the improvements/changes required.

ACTIVITY 11

Stop and consider

What improvements or changes do you need to make to your coaching practice?

1 In the left-hand column of the table below, list the things you can change immediately or in the short term.

2 In the right-hand column, list the improvements and/or changes that might take longer to sort out. Some examples have been given to start you off.

Short-term Improvements/Changes	Long-term Improvements/Changes
Things I can change immediately: • Use appropriate language and terminology so I don't upset or offend participants. • Make sure I don't stereotype people, but am open-minded.	Things I can change in the long term: • Set up a coaching programme to encourage more people from local ethnic minority communities to take part in my sport. • Encourage my club to provide better facilities for disabled people.

3 Now you have identified the short- and long-term improvements/changes that need to be made to your coaching practice, try to put an equity action plan together:

    a   Select the three most important improvements/changes you listed in each column of the table above.

    b   Use the blank action plans provided overleaf to help you identify:

        –   how you intend to make each improvement/change

        –   the date by which you intend to do it.

4 Review your action plans regularly and record your achievements. No doubt you will think of new improvements/changes to add to your list in the future.

A blank copy of the action plans is provided in Appendix G (page 143) for you to photocopy and use as and when required.

SHORT-TERM IMPROVEMENTS/CHANGES		
What?	How?	When?
1		
2		
3		

LONG-TERM IMPROVEMENTS/CHANGES		
What?	How?	When?
1		
2		
3		

7.4 Summary

You should now have identified areas for improvement in your coaching practice and started to put together an equity action plan, whether it be specifically for your own coaching or for your club in general.

Working through this resource may have raised issues you have never previously considered in your coaching. These could include new ideas, training and the need for updating knowledge and current practice. Section Eight provides a comprehensive list of useful contacts, references and recommended reading.

8.0 Introduction

Part of being a good coach is being open to new ideas and training and, to some extent, being aware that you need updating in certain areas. It is also about understanding the needs of the people you are coaching and accepting advice on how to accommodate them. This section provides a comprehensive list of publications, workshops and organisations that can provide support and guidance on equity-related issues.

8.1 Further Reading/Workshops

This section lists a selection of useful publications and workshops that support the information provided in this resource. It is divided into subsections (one for each protected characteristic, plus a miscellaneous section) to make it easier to find the resource(s) you are looking for.

> The Disability Rights Commission, Commission for Racial Equality and the Equal Opportunities Commission, and their guidance documents, are now under the auspices of the EHRC at www.equalityhumanrights.com
>
> The EHRC has published the *Equality Act Starter Kit*, which provides accessible and useful information around the Equality Act both for employers and service providers. Further details can be found on their website, as above.

Disabled People

Davis, R. (2002) *Inclusion Through Sports – A Guide to Enhancing Sport Experiences*. Champaign, Illinois, USA: Human Kinetics. ISBN: 978-0736034-39-5.

English Federation of Disability Sport: 'Disability Sport Events', www.disabilitysport.org.uk

English Federation of Disability Sport (2004) 'EFDS Count Me In: Development Framework (2004–2008)', www.efds.net/content/news/EFDS%20Brochure%20.pdf

Fitzgerald, H. (2011) *Inclusive Coaching: Disability*. Leeds: Coachwise Ltd/The National Coaching Foundation. ISBN: 978-1-905540-87-7.

For the latest disability sport news and research articles, log on to www.efds.co.uk

For advice and guidance on the English Federation of Disability Sport's Inclusive Fitness Initiative (IFI) and to access audits for facilities, accessible fitness equipment, training and marketing, log on to www.inclusivefitness.org

Kerr, A. and Stafford, I. (2005) *Coaching Disabled Performers*. Leeds: Coachwise Business Solutions. ISBN: 978-1-902523-60-6.

Leonard Cheshire and Scope (2006) 'Can-do Volunteering', www.can-do-volunteering.org

Murray, P. (2002) *Hello! Are You Listening? Disabled Teenagers' Experience of Access to Inclusive Leisure*. London: Joseph Rowntree Foundation. ISBN: 978-1-842630-74-7

Royal National Institute for Blind People (2005) *Fit for All: Including Children with Sight Problems in Sport*. Leeds: Coachwise Business Solutions. ISBN: 978-1-858786-44-5.

Scott Porter Research and Marketing Ltd (2000) 'Sport and People with a Disability: aiming at social inclusion', *Research Digest*, 57, www.sportscotland.org.uk

Shelley, P. (2002) *Everybody Here? Play and Leisure for Disabled Children and Young People*. London: Contact a Family. ISBN: 978-1874715-38-2.

Sport England (2000) 'Disability Survey 2000 – Young People with a Disability & Sport', www.sportengland.org

Sport England (2002) 'Access for Disabled People', www.sportengland.org

Sport England (2002) 'Adults with a Disability and Sport National Survey 2000–2001', www.sportengland.org

Sport England (2005) 'Sport and Recreation for People with Disabilities', www.sportengland.org

Workshops

- **sports coach UK:**

  - How to Coach Disabled People in Sport: a two-hour theory workshop aimed at Level 1 and entry level coaches to raise disability awareness around coaching.

  - Inclusive Coaching: Disability: a three-hour part-theory, part-practical workshop to develop the knowledge of Level 2 and above coaches around inclusion of disabled people and the integration of more talented disabled people into competitive disability sport. The one-hour practical session involves coaching a local disability group.

- **EFDS**

  - Including Disabled Pupils in Physical Education

  - Inclusive Training Disability Equality Course

  - The UK Disability Inclusion Training (UK DIT) course: developed by all four home nation disability sport organisations (EFDS, SDS, DSW, DSNI), a one-day course, part-theory, part-practical; sponsorship provided by Typhoo to EFDS to roll out the course to coaches in England.

- **Disability Sports NI**

  - Inclusive Skills: This 3½-hour course provides teachers and leaders with the knowledge and resources required to run a series of warm-up activities, core skills sessions and fun games for disabled and non-disabled children aged five years and over. The course has been specifically designed to meet the needs of teachers and leaders with little or no sporting background, as well as those with formal PE backgrounds. Based on the Sport Northern Ireland (SNI) approved Long-term Athlete Development (LTAD) model, the course focuses on the FUNdamental stage of the model, developing skills such as: movement; balance; catching and throwing; hitting and striking; and kicking. Emphasis is placed on how to adapt the activities for children with physical, sensory or learning disabilities. On completion of the course, all participants will receive the 'Inclusive Skills' resource pack, containing 31 colourful resource cards as well as a Disability Sports NI Certificate of Attendance.

  - Inclusive Games: This 3½-hour course is designed for those currently working, or planning to work, with children or adults with disabilities. Through a series of practical hands-on sessions, participants are provided with enough knowledge to run activity sessions in a range of inclusive games/sports in which disabled and non-disabled children and adults can participate. No previous sports experience is necessary. The inclusive games covered in the course are:

    - boccia

    - goalball

    - table-top games

    - new age kurling

    - zone hockey

    - zone football

    - tee rounders.

On completion of the course, all participants will receive an 'Inclusive Games' resources pack as well as a Disability Sports NI Certificate of Attendance.

For further information or to discuss your training needs contact Disability Sports NI:

Tel: 028-9038 7062, Fax: 028 9038 7063, email@dsni.co.uk

People from Black and Minority Ethnic Communities

Many of the Sporting Equals fact sheets are currently being reviewed. For the most up-to-date details regarding these, contact Sporting Equals using the address on page 126.

Asians in Football Forum (2005) 'Asians Can Play Football. Another Wasted Decade', www.equalityhumanrights.com

Commission for Racial Equality (1999) 'The Stephen Lawrence Inquiry – Implications for Racial Equality', www.equalityhumanrights.com

Commission for Racial Equality (2000) *Achieving Racial Equality: A Standard for Sport*. London: Commission for Racial Equality. ISBN: 978-1-854422-33-0.

Commission for Racial Equality (2002) 'Code of Practice on the Duty to Promote Race Equality', www.equalityhumanrights.com

Commission for Racial Equality (2004) 'Goal – Racial Equality in Football. Summary of Research Findings and Action Plan', www.equalityhumanrights.com

Commission for Racial Equality (2006) 'Employment and Ethnicity' (Factfile 1), www.equalityhumanrights.com

Ploszajski Lynch (2005) 'Increasing BME Participation in Sport & Physical Activity by Black and Ethnic Minority Communities', www.sportdevelopment.org.uk/ menter_bmesports.pdf

Sport England (2000) 'Sports Participation and Ethnicity in England: National Survey 1999/2000 Headline Findings', www.sportengland.org

Sporting Equals (no date) 'Positive Images in Sports Publicity: Sporting Equals Factsheet 1', www.sportingequals.com

Sporting Equals (no date) 'Data Collection: Sporting Equals Factsheet 3', www.sportingequals.com

Sporting Equals (no date) 'Working with Ethnic Minority Communities: Sporting Equals Factsheet 4', www.sportingequals.com

Sporting Equals (no date) 'Developing Racial Equality Policies: Sporting Equals Factsheet 6', www.sportingequals.com

Sporting Equals (no date) 'Representation on Committees: Sporting Equals Factsheet 7', www.sportingequals.com

Sporting Equals (no date) 'Developing Regional Racial Equality Sports Projects: Sporting Equals Factsheet 13' www.sportingequals.com

Sporting Equals (2000) 'Racial Equality Charter', www.sportingequals.com

Sporting Equals (2005) 'Mapping of Ethnic Minority Communities in England', www.sportingequals.com

Sporting Equals (2005) 'Identification of Migrant, Refugee and Asylum Seeker Communities within England', www.sportingequals.com

Sporting Equals (2005) 'Identification of Workforce and Volunteer Profiles within Sports Organisations', www.sportingequals.com

Women's Sport and Fitness Foundation (2006) 'Muslim Women in Sport: A Minority Within a Minority', www.wsf.org.uk/documents/Muslim_women_in_Sport.pdf

Women and Girls

The Equal Opportunities Commission and its plethora of guidance documents are now under the auspices of the EHRC at www.equalityhumanrights.com

Biddle, S., Coalter, F., Donovan, T., MacBeth, J., Nevill, M. and Whitehead, S. (2005) 'Increasing Demand for Sport and Physical Activity by Girls', www.sportscotland.org.uk

Equal Opportunities Commission (1997) 'A Guide to the Sex Discrimination Act 1975', www.equalities.gov.uk

Equal Opportunities Commission (2006) 'Women. Men. Different. Equal. Equal Opportunities Commission', www.equalityhumanrights.com

Equal Opportunities Commission (no date) 'The Sex Discrimination Act and Equal Pay Act', www.equalityhumanrights.com

George Street Research (2004) 'Women in Sport Leadership', www.sportscotland.org.uk

ISRM (no date) 'Single sex sport and leisure provision' (fact sheet), www.isrm.co.uk/policy/PS003_singlesex.pdf

Sport England (2005) 'Determinants of sports and physical activity participation amongst 15–19-year-old young women in England', www.sportengland.org

sports coach UK (2007) 'Women Into High Performance Coaching', www.sportscoachuk.org

sportscotland and Women's Sport and Fitness Foundation (2005) 'Making Women and Girls More Active: A Good Practice Guide', www.sportscotland.org.uk

UK Sport (2004) 'UK Strategy Framework for Women and Sport',
www.uksport.gov.uk/assets/File/Generic_Template_Documents/Standards_in_Sport/equity/Strategy andEquity_Nov03.pdf

UK Sport (2006) 'UK Strategy Framework for Women and Sport – Progress made towards objectives and targets set for 2005 and analysis of the current situation', www.uksport.gov.uk/pages/standards_in_sport_equity/

WomenSport International (no date) 'Sexual Harassment and Abuse of Girls and Women in Sport', www.sportsbiz.bz/womensportinternational/taskforces/wsi_position_statement.htm

Women's Sport and Fitness Foundation offers over 100 different fact sheets, reports and case studies on a wide range of subjects, www.wsff.org.uk

Women's Sport and Fitness Foundation (2009) 'A review of Women's Experiences of Participation in Sport and Other Physical Activity', www.wsff.org.uk

Women's Sport and Fitness Foundation (2010) 'Coaching Female High Performance Athletes', www.wsff.org.uk/publications/fact-sheets/coaching-female-high-performance-athletes

Women's Sport and Fitness Foundation (2011) 'Ultimate Sports Kit for Women', http://wsfftoolkit.org.uk

Workshops

- **Delivered by sports Leaders UK:**
  - WSFF Women, Get Set, Go! (a sport leadership access programme)

Sexual Orientation and Gender Identity

CPSU (2011) 'CPSU Briefing: Homophobic Bullying in Youth Sport', www.nspcc.org.uk/inform/cpsu/resources/briefings/homophobic-bullying-in-youth-sport-wdf81288.pdf

Department for Culture, Media and Sport (2005) 'Transsexual People and Sport – Guidance for Sporting Bodies', www.uksport.gov.uk/assets/File/Generic_Template_Documents/Publications/Standards_in_Sports_Publications/transsexuals.pdf

Pride Sports (2008) 'First National Sports Summit Report', www.vagacms.co.uk/content/showcontent.aspx?contentid=1406

sportscotland (2008) – 'A Literature Review of Sexual Orientation in Sport', www.sportni.net/NR/rdonlyres/1E0DD5D5-6923-444F-BFAO-146FC971F06F/0/A_Literature_Review_of_Sexual_Orientation_in_Sport.pdf

Stonewall (2004) 'The Employment Equality (Sexual Orientation) Regulations Guidelines for Employers', www.stonewall.org.uk/documents/employer_english.pdf

Stonewall (2004) 'Transgender (2004)', www.stonewall.org.uk/documents/BB_Trangender_Booklet.pdf

Stonewall (2006) 'Tuned Out: The BBC's Portrayal of Lesbian and Gay People', www.stonewall.org.uk/documents/tuned_out_pdf.pdf

Age

Long, J. (2004) 'Sport and the Ageing Population: Do Older People have a Place in Driving up Participation in Sport?', www.sportdevelopment.info

Nicholson, L. (2004) 'Older People, Sport and Physical Activity: A Review of Key Issues', ww.sportscotland.org.uk

Sport England (2006) 'Understanding Participation in Sport: What determines sports participation among recently retired people?', www.sportengland.org

Miscellaneous

Sport England has recently revamped its website and, consequently, the URLs of these documents are no longer valid. However, the documents may still be located through the main site at www.sportengland.org

Boocock, S. (2002) 'The Child Protection in Sport Unit', *Journal of Sexual Aggression* (special issue on sexual harassment and abuse in sport), 8: 99–106.

Child Protection in Sport Unit (2006) 'Strategy for Safeguarding Children and Young People in Sport 2006–2012' www.nspcc.org.uk/inform/CPSU/CPSU_wda57648.html

Department for Culture, Media and Sport (2000) 'A sporting future for all', www.sportdevelopment.info

Equality Standard (2004) 'The Equality Standard: A Framework for Sport', www.equalitystandard.org

Equality Standard (2006) 'Scottish Governing Body Support for the Preliminary Level of the Equity Standard', www.equalitystandard.org

Hayes, S. and Stidder, G. (2003) *Equity and Inclusion in Physical Education*. Leeds: Coachwise Business Solutions. ISBN: 978-0-415282-25-3.

Kirby, S. and Wintrup, G. (2002) 'Running the gauntlet in sport: An examination of initiation/hazing and sexual abuse', *Journal of Sexual Aggression* (special issue on sexual harassment and abuse in sport), 8: 49–68.

MORI (2004) *Sports Coaching in the UK*. Leeds: sports coach UK.

NSPCC (2000) *Child Maltreatment in the United Kingdom: A Study of the Prevalence of Child Abuse and Neglect*. London: NSPCC.

Rowe, N. and Champion, R. (2000) *Sports Participation and Ethnicity in England: National Survey 1999/2000 Headline Findings*. London: Sport England. Ref no: SE/1073

Townend, R. and North, J. (2007) *Sports Coaching in the UK II*. Leeds: sports coach UK.

Slinn, N. (2006) *Safeguarding and Protecting Children: a guide for sportspeople*. Leeds: Coachwise Business Solutions. ISBN: 978-0-905540-26-6.

Sneyd, S. (2006) *How to Coach Sports Safely*. Leeds: Coachwise Business Solutions. ISBN: 978-1-902523-50-4.

sports coach UK (2004) 'Sports Coaching in the UK', www.sportscoachuk.org

sports coach UK (2005) *Code of Practice for Sports Coaches* (leaflet). Leeds: Coachwise Business Solutions

Sport England (1999) 'The Value of Sport', www.sportengland.org

Sport England (2000) 'Making English Sport Inclusive: Equity Guidelines for Governing Bodies', www.sportengland.org

Sport England (2002) 'Participation in Sport in England: Sports Equity Index 2002', www.sportengland.org

Sport England (2004) 'The National Framework for Sport in England', www.sportengland.org

Sport England (2006) 'Health and Safety: Hazards, Risk Assessments, Method Statements and COSHH', www.sportengland.org

Sport England (2006) 'No Limits: Sport England's Equity Policy', www.sportengland.org

Sport England (2006) 'Physical Activity and Sport Playing Its Part in Delivering Choosing Health', www.sportengland.org

Sport England (no date) 'Response by Sport England to Consultation White Paper on Fairness for All: A New Commission for Equality and Human Rights', www.sportengland.org

sportscotland (2003) 'Ethics in Sport', www.sportscotland.org.uk

Workshops

- sports coach UK:
    - Equity in Your Coaching
    - Safeguarding and Protecting Children
    - Safeguaring and Protecting Children 2 – reflecting on practice

- running**sports**:
    - A Club for All – knowing your club and its community

8.2 sports coach UK Contacts

sports coach UK

Chelsea Close
Off Amberley Road
Armley
Leeds LS12 4HP

Tel: 0113-274 4802
Fax: 0113-231 9606
Email: coaching@sportscoachuk.org
Website: www.sportscoachuk.org

sports coach UK works closely with governing bodies of sport and other partners to provide a comprehensive service for coaches throughout the UK. This includes an extensive programme of workshops, which have proved valuable to coaches from all types of sports and every level of experience.

For further details of sports coach UK workshops in your area, contact the sports coach UK Workshop Booking Centre:

Tel: 0845-601 3054
Email: scukworkshops@sportscoachuk.org
Website: www.sportscoachuk.org/workshops.php

Details of all sports coach UK publications are available from:

1st4sport.com

Chelsea Close
Off Amberley Road
Armley
Leeds LS12 4HP

Tel: 0113-201 5555
Fax: 0113-231 9606
Email: enquiries@1st4sport.com
Website: www.1st4sport.com

Term	Definition
Bisexual	People who experience sexual attraction towards, and responsiveness to, both males and females. A bisexual person.
Disadvantage	As a result of discrimination (see definition below), some groups are deprived of all or some resources.
Discrimination	**Direct discrimination** Treating people less favourably because of their age, gender, race, disability, nationality, sexual orientation, religion or philosophical belief than others in similar circumstances. **Indirect discrimination** This can occur when following a rule or condition. It appears that all people are treated the same, regardless of protected characteristic, but where it becomes apparent that people of a particular strand suffer or are more likely to suffer a disadvantage. The rule or condition in this instance cannot be justified.
Empowerment	Providing people with the knowledge, information and skills to enable them to have more control over decisions that affect their lives.
Ethnic group	Distinct groups identifiable by a combination of factors, including race, common nationality, traits, customs, culture and traditions[16].
Gay	Males who experience a sexual attraction towards, and responsiveness to, other males. A homosexual male.
Gender equality	Equal status, rights and responsibility for men and women.
Harassment	Inappropriate actions, behaviour, comments or physical contact that is objectionable or causes offence to the recipient. It may be directed towards people because of their gender, appearance, race, colour, ethnic origin, nationality, age, sexual preference, a disability, or some other characteristic.

[16] Definition from *Clean Bowl Racism: A Report on Racial Equality in Cricket*. Reproduced with the kind permission of the ECB Racism Study Group.

Term	Definition
Homophobia	The irrational fear of homosexuals, homosexuality or any behaviour, belief or attitude of self or others that doesn't conform to rigid sex-role stereotypes. It is the fear that enforces sexism and heterosexism.
Institutional racism	The Macpherson Report[17] defines institutional racism as: *The collective failure of an organisation to provide an appropriate and professional service to people because of their colour, culture or ethnic origin. It can be seen or detected in processes, attitudes and behaviour which amount to discrimination through unwitting prejudice, ignorance, thoughtlessness and racist stereotyping, which disadvantage minority ethnic people.* This definition can be applied to all disadvantaged groups who are discriminated against.
Lesbian	Females who experience a sexual attraction towards, and responsiveness to, other females. A homosexual female.
Minority ethnic	An ethnic group within a society or region that is smaller in numbers than the majority population. A minority population is often a group of people whose members have significantly less control or power over their lives than members of the majority group[18].
Positive action	Positive action refers to a variety of measures designed to counteract the effects of past discrimination and to help eliminate stereotyping. Positive action is lawful and, as such, requires an evidence base to justify actions. This could include gaps identified by research, audits or monitoring data.
Positive discrimination	Arising when a disadvantaged individual or group is singled out and treated more favourably than others. Positive discrimination is illegal. For example, a governing body of sport may feel that a particular group of people is under-represented among its registered coaches. Positive discrimination would occur if the governing body of sport proceeded to appoint people from this group without considering others who were better qualified.
Prejudice	Describing negative feelings, thoughts and attitudes people have about other people that have no rational basis. Often ill-considered or preconceived and showing bias towards certain groups of people. Everyone has prejudices about all kinds of things (eg food, clothes).

[17] Macpherson, W. (1999) *The Stephen Lawrence Inquiry: Report of an Inquiry by Sir William Macpherson of Cluny.* London: The Stationery Office. Cm 4262-I.

[18] Definition from *Clean Bowl Racism: A Report on Racial Equality in Cricket.* Reproduced with the kind permission of the ECB Racism Study Group.

Term	Definition
Race	A group of individuals within a biological species. Groups of humans with distinct physical characteristics, such as skin colour and physical features[19].
Racial discrimination	There are three main types of unlawful racial discrimination[20]: **Direct discrimination** When someone is treated less favourably on racial grounds than other people in the same or a similar situation. **Indirect discrimination** When there is a rule or condition that applies to everybody, but people from a certain racial group are not able to meet it and there is no justifiable reason for having that rule. **Victimisation** When someone may be targeted for making a complaint of discrimination under the Race Relations Act 1976 and the Race Relations (Amendment Act) 2000.
Racial equality	Equal status, rights and responsibilities for people of different racial groups.
Stereotyping	Grouping or labelling people because they share a particular trait(s), which is regarded as characteristic of that group. Stereotyping is usually negative and is frequently used to justify discrimination.
Transgender	Transsexual people have the deep conviction that the gender to which they were assigned at birth on the basis of their physical anatomy (referred to as their 'birth gender') is incorrect. That conviction will often lead them to take steps to present themselves to the world as the opposite gender. Often, transsexual people will undergo hormonal or surgical treatment to bring their physical identity into line with their preferred gender identity.

[19] Definition from *Clean Bowl Racism: A Report on Racial Equality in Cricket*. Reproduced with the kind permission of the ECB Racism Study Group.

[20] Commission for Racial Equality (1998) *Racial Discrimination is Against the Law – Campaign to Increase Young People's Awareness of Their Rights Under the Race Relations Act*. Campaigns Pack. London: Commission for Racial Equality.

The government has recognised the value of sport in promoting the inclusion of all groups of people in society, and as part of programmes to reduce crime and antisocial behaviour. The government agenda in relation to equity in society in general also applies to sport. As a result, many initiatives and organisations have been introduced to improve the sporting opportunities available to people from the protected characteristics. This appendix provides a summary of the key organisations and initiatives you should be aware of. It is divided into the following four sections:

- **Government Agenda** takes a look at key government initiatives designed to provide better sporting opportunities for disabled people, people from minority ethnic communities and women and girls.

- **Sports Agenda** examines the progress made by key UK sports organisations.

- **Coaching Agenda** looks at coaching-specific initiatives.

- **Equality Agenda** looks at equality agendas across the UK.

This appendix will help you look at the **bigger picture** beyond government policy and understand why sports equity in coaching is so important.

Government Agenda

A Sporting Future for All (2000)

In April 2000, the government launched a new sports strategy entitled A Sporting Future for All. This strategy seeks to give a lead in creating a more coordinated approach to improving sporting opportunities for all sections of the community and improving performance in international competitions. More specifically, it aims to improve the opportunities for disabled people, people from minority ethnic communities, and girls and women, to participate, lead, coach and officiate in sport.

Coaches have a central role to play in A Sporting Future for All. The strategy aims to ensure coaches of sufficient quality and quantity are available from the grass roots of sport to the international arena.

A Sporting Future for All can be viewed online at the DCMS website: www.culture.gov.uk

Policy Action Team 10 (PAT 10): A Report to the Social Exclusion Unit (1999)

Policy Action Team 10 (PAT 10): A Report to the Social Exclusion Unit recommends sport be used as part of programmes to reduce crime and antisocial behaviour. It also highlights the need for an increase in the number of people from disadvantaged groups taking part in sport. This can only happen if sport is seen by these groups to be equitable and available to them.

PAT 10: A Report to the Social Exclusion Unit can be viewed online at the DCMS website: www.culture.gov.uk

Social Inclusion – Opening the Door to a Better Scotland (1999)

This report, published by the Scottish Office in 1999, highlights the potential role of sport in promoting social inclusion. The Scottish Executive's aim is to increase participation in sport by people at all age and ability levels, and to encourage young people to remain active in sport as they enter and progress through adulthood. Through **sport**scotland, the Scottish Executive will encourage improved access to sport by promoting equality of opportunity, whether the inequality is linked to poverty, geographical isolation, race or gender discrimination, or disability.

Social Inclusion – Opening the Door to a Better Scotland can be viewed online at The Scottish Executive's website: www.scotland.gov.uk

The Macpherson Report (1999)

This is the report of the Stephen Lawrence Inquiry. The report found that institutional racism played a part in the flawed investigation by the Metropolitan Police into the murder of Stephen Lawrence. The Macpherson Report defines institutional racism as:

> The collective failure of an organisation to provide an appropriate and professional service to people because of their colour, culture or ethnic origin. It can be seen or detected in processes, attitudes and behaviour which amount to discrimination through unwitting prejudice, ignorance, thoughtlessness and racist stereotyping, which disadvantage minority ethnic people.
>
> The Macpherson Report (1999)[21]

As a result of the Macpherson Report and recommendations made by the Commission for Racial Equality (now under the auspices of the EHRC), the Race Relations (Amendment) Act 2000 was introduced to extend the Race Relations Act 1976 to a wide range of public authorities.

The Brighton Declaration (1994)

The first international conference on women and sport took place in Brighton in 1994. Aimed at decision makers from governmental and non-governmental sectors, it focused entirely on women and sport. There were three main outcomes from the conference:

- an International Strategy on Women and Sport
- the Brighton Declaration
- the creation of the International Working Group on Women and Sport (IWG).

The Brighton Declaration is addressed to all governments and organisations that are responsible for, or have some influence over, women in sport. It complements all other laws, charters, codes and rules relating to women and/or sport and provides a comprehensive set of principles for the development of opportunities for women and sport. Its overriding aim is:

> to develop a sporting culture that enables and values the full involvement of women in every aspect of sport.
>
> Women and sport and the challenge of change
> (Sport England, 1994)

The Brighton Declaration can be viewed online at the IWG's website: www.iwg-gti.org

A World Conference on Women and Sport is held each year. For further information, visit www.iwg-gti.org

---

[21] Macpherson, W. (1999) *The Stephen Lawrence Inquiry: Report of an Inquiry by Sir William Macpherson of Cluny.* London, The Stationery Office. Cm 4262-I.

Game Plan: A Strategy for Delivering Government's Sport and Physical Activity Objectives

Published in December 2002, this comprehensive document was produced jointly by the government's Strategy Unit and the DCMS.

With sections that include comparative participation and sports performance data, research statistics and theories underpinning the value of sport (such as they are), it details the government's vision and strategy for sport from both a mass participation and performance perspective up until 2020.

This document was published prior to the awarding of The London 2012 Olympic Games and Paralympic Games.

Game Plan was larger and more comprehensive than any other recent 'sport policy' documents, and sought to provide statistics and comment about sport participation and the inequalities associated with it, to give a rationale for plans to reduce these inequalities.

It also attempted to provide both a rationale and an action plan for the development of sport itself, and the reduction of social exclusion, by providing opportunities in sport participation, based largely on the claims made for sport in the social exclusion unit's PAT 10 report. Game Plan made suggestions towards sport being a potential instrument in achieving the government's wider socio-political agenda of combating social exclusion.

Game Plan articulated a clear statement that government perceived sport and physical activity as a potential social instrument, to reduce the inequalities of opportunities for people (citizens) to participate in the social structures of British society.

Game Plan can be viewed online at: www.cabinetoffice.gov.uk

Every Child Matters

Every Child Matters is the government's scheme outlining five outcomes key to well-being in childhood and later life. They are:

- being healthy
- staying safe
- enjoying and achieving
- making a positive contribution
- achieving economic well-being.

The government's aim is to improve on these outcomes for all children.

Every Child Matters can be viewed online at: www.everychildmatters.org

Sports Agenda

Equality Standard for Sport

The Equality Standard for Sport (the Standard) is a framework and vehicle for widening access and increasing the participation and involvement in sport and physical activity of under-represented individuals, groups and communities, especially women and girls, people from minority ethnic communities and disabled people. It will assist sports organisations in developing equality-proofed policies, structures and processes, and will allow for performance to be assessed, ensuring continuous improvement in equality.

The Standard is a collaboration of the four Home Country Sports Councils and UK Sport, and is supported by the Central Council of Physical Recreation (CCPR), the WSFF, the EFDS and Sporting Equals. Progress through the Standard is a mandatory condition within the national funding agreements involving Sport England, governing bodies of sport, and national and regional sports organisations in England. For those governing bodies of sport with a UK-wide remit, UK Sport has linked the achievement of each level within the Standard with models of good governance, as outlined in its specific initiative, Investing in Change.

The Standard Explained

The Standard is based on two broad areas of activity:

- **Developing Your Organisation**
  This will be a reflection of the culture, policies, leadership and people of your organisation.

- **Developing Your Services**
  This refers to the impact policies, leadership and people have on an organisation's programmes, communications and customer service. It encompasses the four levels of achievement: Foundation, Preliminary, Intermediate and Advanced.

Foundation

The organisation is committed to equality, and that commitment is communicated to all staff and volunteers.

Preliminary

The organisation is clear about what it needs to do to achieve equality. It understands the issues and barriers faced by under-represented groups in sport, and has a robust equality action plan that all staff, volunteers and key stakeholders understand.

Intermediate

The organisation is increasing opportunities for participation and involvement by a diverse range of people, including representation of its own leadership, staff, board and senior volunteers. All internal policies pay due regard to diversity.

Advanced

Leadership and staff (including coaches and officials), as well as participants, are offered a fair and equal opportunity, and are reflective of the community the organisation serves. Equality is central to the way an organisation carries out all of its work. All affiliated organisations and clubs are able to engage and develop participants, coaches, officials and administrators from under-represented groups.

Assessment and Verification of Achievements

Following the pilot scheme, the Sport Council Equity Group (SCEG) has reviewed the Equality Standard Strategy and, more significantly, the assessment and verification process involved. The review has resulted in a more efficient and practical approach.

Equality Standard Advisors - ESA

Equality Standard Advisors (ESAs) have been recruited, trained and deployed by the relevant home country to provide one-to-one support for governing bodies of sport or CSPs. The ESA is responsible for assessing a governing body of sport's progress against the outcomes set within the Standard.

The ESA and the organisation will be required to plan the support that will be needed over a three-day period. This will be set out in a contract and the time allocated accordingly. The ESA will produce a report detailing the reasons why he/she is of the opinion the organisation has met the essential criteria for the relevant level

Equality Standard Verifiers

Equality Standard Verifiers (ESVs) will be responsible for independently verifying the assessment process and report carried out by the ESA. There will be two ESVs allocated for each assessment on a cross-home-country basis.

This process will replace the current panel and will continue to operate on a quarterly basis. The ESVs will contact the ESA, requesting any evidence required to validate the information contained within the report before making a final decision. If necessary, the ESV can also contact the governing body of sport or CSP directly. There are only two possible outcomes from this process for the sports organisation. It has either achieved, or is still working towards, a level and is directed to address the areas of development that have been identified. The relevant sports council will confirm the decision and communicate this to the ESA.

Each Home Country Sports Council will coordinate its own assessment process. UK Sport will coordinate those governing bodies of sport with a UK remit.

Sports Council Equity Group

Sports equity is coordinated on a UK-wide basis through SCEG. This group is made up of UK Sport and the four Home Country Sports Councils. The purpose of this group is to:

- work more collaboratively across the UK (between sports councils)
- widen the equality agenda
- ensure training takes place in the area of equality
- annually set dates in advance for effective meetings.

The terms of reference for SCEG are to:

- agree work priorities in all areas of equity and inclusion across the UK
- work collaboratively to influence the sports agenda in the UK
- promote consistency in implementing collaborative or common projects
- share expertise, good practice and relevant experience
- lead the strategic development and implementation of the Equality Standard
- engage and consult with relevant agencies to ensure effective implementation of equity and inclusion in the UK.

The Sports Council Equity Group Model

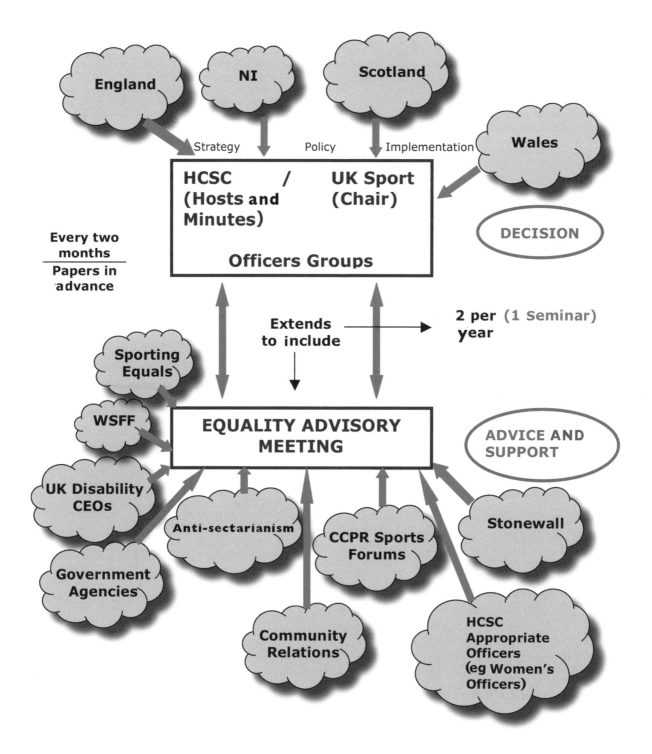

Sport England

3rd Floor, Victoria House
Bloomsbury Square
London WC1B 4SE

Tel: 0845-8508 508
Fax: 020-7383 5740
Email: info@sportengland.org
Website: www.sportengland.org

Sport England is the government agency responsible for building the foundations of sporting success, by creating a world-leading community sport system of clubs, coaches, facilities and volunteers.

Formerly known as the English Sports Council, Sport England works in partnership with UK Sport, which has responsibility for elite success, and the Youth Sport Trust (YST), which is focused on physical education and school sport.

Accountable to Parliament through the DCMS, Sport England has a role protecting sports provision as a statutory consultee on planning applications that affect playing fields. Sport England must be consulted if community playing fields are threatened by potential developments.

Sport England invests expertise, resources and both government and Lottery money into community sport – £480million is invested directly through 46 governing bodies of sport. There are five open funding streams other organisations can apply to.

A wealth of expertise and advice is provided on a range of sports subjects, including planning, facilities, coaching, volunteering and sports development.

Sport England is a strong advocate for community sport, bringing together a wide range of partners from local and national government, the commercial sector, Further Education (FE) and Higher Education (HE), and the third sector, to make the most of its investment in sport.

These partners include:

- sporting landscape partners YST and UK Sport

- governing bodies of sport

- national partners, including three main sports equality organisations (EFDS, WSFF and Sporting Equals)

- local authorities

- CSPs

- FE and HE

- the third sector

- the commercial sector

- The London Organising Committee of the Olympic and Paralympic Games (LOCOG) and the Olympic Delivery Authority (ODA).

As stated above, Sport England's focus is around three outcomes – **growing, sustaining** the numbers of people taking part in sport, and improving talent development to help more people **excel**.

It has five targets that will assist in delivering these outcomes:

Grow

- One million people taking part in more sport.

- More children and young people taking part in five hours of physical education and sport a week.

These targets account for 15% of its investment.

Sustain

- More people satisfied with their sporting experience.

- 25% fewer 16–18 year olds dropping out of at least five sports.

These targets account for 60% of its investment.

Excel

- Improved talent development in at least 25 sports.

This target accounts for 25% of its investment.

sportscotland

Doges
Templeton on the Green
62 Templeton Street
Glasgow G40 IDA

Tel: 0141-534 6500
Fax: 0141-534 6501
Email: sportscotland.enquiries@sportscotland.org.uk
Website: www.sportscotland.org.uk

A Vision for Equity in Scottish Sport

The vision for Scottish sport is for Scotland to be
a country:

- where sport is more widely available to all

- where sporting talent is recognised and nurtured

- that achieves and sustains world-class performance
  in sport.

At the core of this vision is the principle of sport for all.
This means all Scottish residents, regardless of ability,
ethnic group, gender, age, background, sexuality and
marital or civil partnership status, should have equal
opportunities, not only to participate in sport
recreationally, but also to develop talent and
achieve excellence.

Underpinning the vision to transform Scotland into a
truly sporting nation, as set out in the national strategy
for sport, are the dual challenges of increasing
participation and improving performance. Rising to meet
these challenges will be critical to the successful
achievement of the vision for Scottish sport.

One of the key aims of **sport**scotland's corporate plan is
to increase participation in Scottish sport. To help
achieve this aim, **sport**scotland has identified the need to
work with its partners to increase participation by
people from a number of target groups, including:

- women and girls

- disabled people

- people from minority ethnic communities.

sportscotland's Work on Equity

sportscotland published its **Single Equity Scheme** ('the
Scheme') on 4 December 2006. The Scheme is an
integrated strategy and action plan, which sets out
sportscotland's planned work in equity over the
period from December 2006 to December 2009. It
sets out how **sport**scotland will fulfil its public sector
duties to promote disability, equality, race equality and
gender equality.

sportscotland, in partnership with other sports councils
in the UK, is committed to the roll-out of the **Equality
Standard: A Framework for Sport** ('the Standard').
sportscotland achieved the Foundation level of the
Equality Standard in June 2006, and supported 12 pilot
Scottish governing bodies towards achievement of the
Standard during 2005–2007. **sport**scotland remains
committed to supporting the Scottish governing bodies
to achieve the Standard, and to achieving further levels
of the Standard itself.

sportscotland is also very active in terms of work in
relation to specific equity areas. It works in close
partnership with Scottish Disability Sport to develop
disability sport in Scotland, and with the WSFF to develop
sport and physical recreation for women and girls.

In addition, it has also produced a brochure that
provides an overview of the key areas of ethics in
sport. This brochure can be accessed by visiting
www.sportscotland.org.uk (the website also contains a
wealth of information about ethics in sport and, more
specifically, equity).

Sport Northern Ireland

House of Sport
2a Upper Malone Road
Belfast BT9 5LA

Tel: 028-9038 1222
Fax: 028-9068 2757
Email: info@sportni.net
Website: www.sportni.net

Sport Northern Ireland (Sport NI) is committed to providing equality of opportunity for everyone who wishes to participate in sport to the level of their choice, with due regard for the need to promote equality of opportunity between:

- persons of different religious belief, political opinion, racial background, age, marital status or sexual orientation

- men and women generally

- persons with a disability and persons without

- persons with dependants and persons without.

Sport NI will continue to examine ways of increasing opportunities for people who are under-represented in sport to access sport to the level of their choice. It reviews and screens all policies and programmes to ensure equality of opportunity for all, in accordance with Section 75 of the Northern Ireland Act 1998.

In working towards achieving this objective, Sport NI has:

- developed and adopted a Sports Equity Policy and a Disability Mainstreaming Policy

- developed a range of sports equity courses and resources designed to support sports clubs and organisations in working towards equality

- played a role in the development and implementation of the UK Equality Standard for Sport.

Sport Wales

Sophia Gardens
Cardiff CF11 9SW

Tel: 0845-045 0904
Fax: 0845-846 0014
Email: scw@scw.org.uk
Website: www.sports-council-wales.org.uk

Sport Wales is committed to the promotion of equity and diversity and works to ensure all people and communities have access to sport.

Child Protection and Equity

Sport Wales has in place a dedicated child protection and equity officer. Part of this role is to implement, monitor and evaluate ethics and equity policies and practices within Welsh governing bodies of sport.

Equality Standard

Sport Wales forms a key part of SCEG, which consists of a representative from each home country. SCEG works to develop a coordinated approach to equality across sports councils in the UK and has developed the Equality Standard for Sport, which is the first of its kind. The Standard has been developed to widen access and reduce inequalities in sport and physical exercise.

In addition to the overarching equity work carried out by Sport Wales, there are a number of specific projects and initiatives that have been developed and are supported by the council to target under-represented groups in sport.

Women and Girls

A women and girls' sport forum has been established since 2001 and meets regularly across the country. This allows Sport Wales to report on progress being made and advise on how it can improve its programmes, and influence its partners and the existing infrastructure of sport to respond to the needs of women and girls.

Disability

The Federation of Disability Sport Wales (FDSW) works alongside Sport Wales in a joint commitment to the provision of high-quality education and training for coaches and volunteers working within disability sport. This continued development of inclusive coach education leads to increased sporting opportunities for all individuals, regardless of their disability status.

Young People

Through the Active Young People programmes, Sport Wales has invested in developing young people's participation and will create long-term cultural change and lifelong habits leading to health gains, as well as increasing participation in sport. Young people have been the focus of much of the work of Sport Wales for many years.

Minority Ethnic Communities

All Sport Wales' programmes offer the opportunity for all communities to overcome the barriers affecting participation in sport and physical activity. These are magnified in areas where there are large minority ethnic communities. Corporately, Sport Wales has put in place the Race Equality Scheme, which is supported by a yearly action plan. On the ground, officers are striving to create stronger links with minority ethnic communities through engagement, representation and communication.

Socially Disadvantaged Groups

Many areas of Wales are characterised by large pockets of social and economic deprivation. Sport and physical activity have a key role to play in promoting better health, social inclusion and community cohesion in these areas. A fundamental aim of Sport Wales' Active Communities project is to invest in Wales' most recreationally and socio-economically deprived communities and Communities First areas, to develop sport and physical activity participation and support community regeneration.

UK Sport

40 Bernard Street
London WC1N 1ST

Tel: 020-7211 5100
Fax: 020-7211 5246
Email: info@uksport.gov.uk
Website: www.uksport.gov.uk

UK Sport aims to promote the highest standards of sporting conduct and explore sport's wider social applications.

Initiatives include working with athletes, officials and key partners to promote the highest standards of conduct and fair play, both on and off the field of play. In addition, UK Sport takes a leading role in promoting equality in sport to ensure there are no barriers to participation and involvement in the running of sport for any social groups.

The overall aim is to support the development of a fair, equitable and ethical world-class sporting system in the UK that is athlete-centred and people-focused.

UK Sport embraces the spirit of all equality legislation and is committed to eradicating any form of unfair discrimination. UK Sport will not tolerate discrimination, either directly or indirectly, on the grounds of race, disability, class or social background, religious belief, sexual orientation, ethnic or national origin, gender, marital or parental status, pregnancy, age, colour or political persuasion.

UK Sport is committed to achieving equality in sport and is taking a proactive approach in this area. It is a central principle of a dynamic and modern sports organisation that can demonstrate democratic governance with progressive strategies and programmes.

To underline its commitment, UK Sport leads on the following:

- Women and Leadership Development Programme – UK Sport is committed to gender equality in sport and recognises that the situation for women in leadership is such that positive action is required. The programme provides training and support for women with the talent and desire to achieve senior positions in sport. The programme not only reaffirms UK Sport's commitment to gender equality, but also contributes to worldwide impact goals in terms of international representation and advancing world-class standards, by improving governance in sport.

- The Equality Standard: A Framework for Sport – the Standard is a framework to guide sport and community organisations towards achieving equality. It will assist organisations in developing structures and processes, assessing performance and ensuring continuous improvement in equality.

- Paralympic World Class Pathway – this supports Paralympic athletes through the three key levels of the pathway: World Class Talent, Development and Podium.

- Ethical research – one element of UK Sport's 100% ME programme is ethical research into attitudes surrounding doping. UK Sport has previously carried out research into ethics in sport, primarily focused on fair play at high-profile events.

Disability

Disability Sport Wales

Sport Wales National Centre
Sophia Gardens
Cardiff CF11 9SW

Tel: 0845-846 0021
Fax: 029-2066 5781
Email: office@fdsw.org.uk
Website: www.disabilitysportwales.org

Disability Sport Wales embraces two new schemes:

- National Performance Scheme
- Local Development Scheme.

The schemes aim to increase participation among disabled people and improve opportunities for talented disabled competitors to fulfil their potential. They are managed by two national officers coordinated by the Federation of Sports Associations for the Disabled (FSAD) and the Sports Council for Wales.

Disability Sports Northern Ireland

Adelaide House
Falcon Road
Belfast BT12 6SJ

Tel: 028-9038 7062
Email: email@dsni.co.uk
Website: www.dsni.co.uk

Disability Sports Northern Ireland is the national umbrella body responsible for the coordination, promotion and development of sport for disabled people throughout Northern Ireland. It has initiated and organised a range of projects and works closely with sports providers and governing bodies of sport to promote the inclusion of people with disabilities in mainstream sport.

English Federation of Disability Sport

SportPark
Loughborough University
3 Oakwood Drive
Loughborough
Leicestershire
LE11 3QF

Tel: 01509-227 750
Fax: 01509-227 777
Email: federation@efds.co.uk
Website: www.efds.co.uk

Launched in 1998, the EFDS is the umbrella organisation for disability sport in England. It brings together the eight National Disability Sport Organisations (NDSOs) recognised by Sport England:

- British Amputees and Les Autres Sports Association
- British Blind Sport
- CP Sport
- Dwarf Athletics
- Mencap Sport
- Special Olympics
- UK Deaf Sport
- WheelPower – British Wheelchair Sport.

The EFDS' mission is:

to be the united voice of disability sport, seeking to promote inclusion and achieve equality of sporting opportunities for disabled people.

The EFDS' objective is to increase participation in sport and ensure disabled people can access the sport and physical activity of their choice, at a level of their choice and a venue of their choice.

The EFDS works at a strategic level, seeking to influence the policies and programmes of those agencies directly and indirectly involved in the provision of opportunities for disabled people in sport and physical activity.

The EFDS plays a key role at a national level in the development of disability sport in this country:

- providing a 'first-stop shop' for advice, guidance and information on disability sport
- actively campaigning and lobbying to raise the profile of disability sport and, in so doing, increasing public awareness of disabled sportswomen and sportsmen
- attracting additional funds to disability sport
- influencing and supporting partners across the delivery system of sport to be more inclusive and provide a greater range and quality of sporting opportunities for disabled people
- working with partners to empower disabled people to take a more active role in all aspects of sport and physical activity – be it as administrator, coach, official, participant, spectator or volunteer
- developing and rolling out programmes such as the **Inclusive Fitness Initiative**, which are designed to improve access to sport and physical activity for disabled people
- through **inclusive training**, providing a range of high-quality training and coaching opportunities designed to increase the number of disabled people involved in sport and physical activity
- providing a comprehensive calendar of major events organised by **Disability Sport Events**, increasing the number of disabled people participating at all levels of the player pathway, and supporting the identification and development of talented performers.

EFDS' Regional Work

The EFDS is committed to improving opportunities for all disabled people to participate in sport and physical activity to the level of their choice. At regional level, the EFDS works with the NDSOs, governing bodies of sport and CSPs to drive forwards the development of disability sport.

The EFDS' regional network of offices is seen as a key part of the overall structure for disability sport in England, providing an accessible point of contact for those involved, or interested, in disability sport at a local level.

The EFDS' regional offices mirror the functions of the organisation nationally, operating at a strategic rather than direct service provision level to:

- provide advice, guidance and information at a local level, highlighting examples of best practice
- facilitate local initiatives and the roll-out of national programmes designed to increase the range and quality of opportunities for disabled people to enjoy sport and physical activity
- enable club development
- empower disabled people
- influence and engage, including working with partners to identify and secure the funding required to ensure programmes and initiatives are sustainable in the long term
- ensure school-club links exist
- support the player pathway
- enable workforce development.

Scottish Disability Sport

Caledonia House
South Gyle
Edinburgh EH12 9DQ

Tel: 0131-317 1130
Fax: 0131-317 1075
Email: admin@scottishdisabilitysport.com
Website: www.scottishdisabilitysport.com

Scottish Disability Sport (SDS) (formerly the Scottish Sports Association for Disabled People [SSAD]) was formed in 1962 to provide facilities for, and to encourage the development of, sport and physical recreation for disabled people.

SDS has in place a strategic plan, Towards London and Beyond 2006–2012, which provides a framework for all its operations. Towards London and Beyond 2006–2012 highlights four strategic goals that influence its work. These goals will:

- support the development of a sporting pathway for young people with physical, sensory or learning disabilities
- encourage and support Scottish athletes with a disability to realise their full potential in sport
- recruit new partners involved in physical activity and/or disability and further develop existing partnerships
- work with regional coaching partnerships to access the very best of education and leadership for athletes and volunteers
- introduce individuals with disabilities to sport through local development programmes at foundation and participation level.

sportscotland invests in SDS and is proud to be a supporter of this positive and proactive organisation.

Ethnicity

Sporting Equals

1301 Stratford Road
Hall Green
Birmingham B28 9HH

Tel: 0121-777 1375
Fax: 0121-325 5477
Email: info@sportingequals.org.uk
Website: www.sportingequals.org.uk

Sporting Equals exists to promote ethnic diversity across sport and physical activity, and is the only organisation in the UK to do so. Set up in 1998 by Sport England, in partnership with the Commission for Racial Equality, but now an independent body, it informs, influences and inspires, in order to create an environment in which:

- black and minority ethnic communities can influence and participate in all aspects of sport and physical activity

- the governors and providers of sport and physical activity recognise and value a fully integrated and inclusive society

- ethnic diversity is recognised and celebrated.

In short, Sporting Equals works proactively for an active world free from racial discrimination and health inequalities, because it is fair, because it is right, and because the whole of society will benefit. Sporting Equals has three objectives:

- To raise awareness and understanding of the needs of black and minority ethnic communities within the sports and health sector, in order to change attitudes and increase participation in sport and physical activity

- To empower individuals and communities to play a part in this change and achieve their full potential through playing sport and being active

- To advise and support policymakers and delivery bodies to be inclusive.

Sporting Equals offers the following services:

- policy advice

- research

- training

- resource development

- independent assessment.

Promoting Racial Equality Through Sport: A Standard for Local Authority Sport and Leisure Services ('the Standard') is designed to assist local authorities in planning, developing and promoting racial equality through the formulation and delivery of their sports provision and services. The Standard has been developed in partnership between the Local Government Association and Sporting Equals.

The Standard will bring further recognition to the value of sport in tackling issues of inequality within communities. It will also provide a tool to assist best value and comprehensive performance assessment frameworks, and help local authorities to meet the general statutory duty as outlined in the Race Relations (Amendment) Act 2000.

Sport for Communities

Sport for Communities was a national initiative managed by Sporting Equals that was funded for three years from 2006–2008 inclusive by the Invest to Save Budget programme, which is sponsored by the DCMS.

It aimed to support the development of integrated sporting activities in inner-city communities, particularly targeted at people from minority ethnic communities, refugee and migrant backgrounds. To enhance this, employment opportunities in sport will be developed with these communities.

The project was managed by Sporting Equals and delivered in partnership with two main groups of agencies that have a national and regional presence – the governing bodies of sport, and local authority sport and leisure services. Local minority ethnic communities, refugees and migrants will also be involved and included as partners.

For a full report on this project, see the Sporting Equals website: www.sportingequals.org.uk

Women and Girls

Women's Sport and Fitness Foundation

3rd Floor, Victoria House
Bloomsbury Square
London WC1B 4SE

Tel: 020-7273 1740
Fax: 020-7273 1981
Email: info@wsff.org.uk
Website: www.wsff.org.uk

The WSFF believes in a society that encourages, enables and celebrates active women and girls. To do this, WSFF will authoritatively and creatively campaign to make:

* sport as appealing to women and girls as it is to men and boys

* women aware of the importance of being active

* fit and healthy women and girls social and cultural role models.

To support this, WSFF will:

* conduct innovative research that can provide insight into the barriers to sport and exercise, and help create the innovative solutions that can overcome them

* work in partnership with the government across sport, health and education, and with business and the media, to inform and influence policy at the highest level

* provide consultancy and advice to those delivering sport and exercise, to help ensure that what they do is designed with women in mind.

Sexuality

Pride Sports

6 Selborne Road
Manchester
M21 0BL

Email: info@pridesports.org
Website: www.pridesports.org

Established in 2006, Pride Sports is the UK's only lesbian, gay, bisexual and transsexual sports development and equity organisation. Pride Sports has two strategic aims:

* to challenge homophobia in sport

* to increase lesbian, gay, bisexual and transsexual participation in sport.

To achieve these aims, Pride Sports delivers a number of initiatives, such as lesbian, gay, bisexual and transsexual sports club development, the delivery of the UK's annual lesbian, gay, bisexual and transsexual multisport festival, Pride Games, as well as:

* policy advice

* training

* resource development

* consultancy

* research

to those delivering sport and physical activity around the UK.

Stonewall

Tower Building
York Road
London SE1 7NX

Tel: 0800-050 2020
Fax: 020-7593 1877
Email: info@stonewall.org.uk
Website: www.stonewall.org.uk

Stonewall was founded in 1989 by a small group of women and men who had been active in the struggle against Section 28 of the Local Government Act.

The aim from the outset was to create a professional lobbying group that would prevent such attacks on lesbians, gay men and bisexuals from ever occurring again. Stonewall has subsequently put the case for equality on the mainstream political agenda, by winning support within all the main political parties, and now has offices in England, Scotland and Wales.

Stonewall is renowned for its campaigning and lobbying. Some major successes include helping achieve the equalisation of the age of consent, lifting the ban on lesbians and gay men serving in the military, securing legislation allowing same-sex couples to adopt, and the repeal of Section 28. More recently, Stonewall has helped secure civil partnerships and ensured the Equality Act 2006 protected lesbians and gay men in terms of goods and services.

Stonewall focuses on the following areas:

- research and policy
- parliamentary issues, including the Equality Bill and other supporting legislation
- publications – on a range of topics, including, hate crime, lesbian health and homophobic bullying in schools
- information service – Stonewall runs a free information service for individuals, organisations and employers
- events – Stonewall runs a number of community and award-style events.

The Gender Trust

Community Base
113 Queens Road
Brighton BN1 3XG

Helpline: 0845-231 0505
Contact: 01273-234 024
Email: info@gendertrust.org.uk
Website: www.gendertrust.org.uk

The Gender Trust is the only registered charity in a position to help adults in the UK who are transsexual, gender dysphoric, transgender (ie those who seek to adjust their lives to live as women or men, or come to terms with their situation despite their genetic background), or those whose lives are affected by gender identity issues.

The Gender Trust's mission is:

to improve the quality of life of trans people and their families, by supporting them and working with anyone who is affected by gender identity issues.

Its vision is:

that everyone will accept and support the right of trans people to be valued members of society.

Age

Age UK

Tavis House
1–6 Tavistock Square
London
WC1H 9NA

Tel: 0800-169 8787
Free helpline: 0800-169 6565
Website: www.ageuk.org.uk

Age UK has a vision of a world in which older people flourish. It aims to improve later life for everyone through its information and advice, campaigns, products, training and research.

Age UK supports and assists a network of over 170 local Age UKs, which between them provide an extensive network throughout England. The Age UK family also includes Age Scotland, Age Cymru and Age NI:

Age Scotland

Causewayside House
160 Causewayside, Edinburgh EH9 1PR

Tel: 0845-125 9732
Email: info@agescotland.org.uk

Age Cymru (Wales)

Tŷ John Pathy
13/14 Neptune Court, Vanguard Way, Cardiff CF24 5PJ

Tel: 029-2043 1555
Email: enquiries@agecymru.org.uk

Age NI (Northern Ireland)

3 Lower Crescent, Belfast BT7 1NR

Tel: 028-9024 5729
Email: info@ageni.org

Values

Age Concern work is also guided by a set of values:

- Enabling – it enables older people to live independently and exercise choice.

- Influential – it draws strength from the voices of older people, and ensures those voices are heard.

- Dynamic – it is innovative and driven by results and constantly delivers for older people.

- Caring – it is passionate about what it does and cares about each individual.

- Expert – it is authoritative, trusted and quality-oriented.

Corporate Priorities 2007–2010

- To prevent poverty and maximise income in retirement.

- To promote age equality and enable older people to make full contributions to our economy, society and neighbourhoods.

- To maximise healthy life expectancy and promote health, independence and well-being for all older people.

- To achieve greater social inclusion of the most disadvantaged older people and challenge the causes of exclusion.

- To achieve a step change in effectiveness and efficiency, in which a crucial element will be a greater focus on older people as customers and contributors to all that we do.

Child Protection in Sport Unit (CPSU)

England

NSPCC National Training Centre
3 Gilmour Close
Beaumont Leys
Leicester LE4 1EZ

Tel: 0116-234 7278
Email: cpsu@nspcc.org.uk
Website: www.thecpsu.org.uk

Northern Ireland

Child Protection in Sport Unit Northern Ireland
NSPCC
Block 1
Jennymount Business Park
North Derby Street
Belfast BT15 3HN

Tel: 028-9035 1135
Email: cpsu@nspcc.org.uk

Wales

Child Protection in Sport Unit Wales
NSPCC Cymru/Wales
Capital Tower
Greyfriars Road
Cardiff CF10 3AG

Tel: 029-2026 7000
Email: cpsuwales@nspcc.org.uk

Scotland

Child Protection in Sport Service
CHILDREN 1ST
Sussex House
61 Sussex Street
Kinning Park
Glasgow G41 1DY

Tel: 0141-418 5674
Email: cpinsport@children1st.org.uk
Web: www.childprotectioninsport.org.uk

The CPSU is a partnership between the NSPCC, Sport England, **sport**scotland, Sport Northern Ireland and the Sports Council for Wales.

The Unit was founded in 2001 to coordinate and support sports organisations' implementation of the 2000 National Action Plan for Child Protection in Sport.

The CPSU works with UK sports councils, governing bodies and other organisations to help them minimise the risk of child abuse during sporting activities.

Mission

To safeguard the welfare of children and young people under 18 years of age in sport, and to promote their well-being.

The CPSU plays an important part in the NSPCC's long-term strategy for ending child abuse by helping sports and other organisations to:

- recognise their responsibility to protect children and young people left in their care

- develop strategies and standards to protect children and young people

- identify and respond to adults who are a threat to children and young people

- develop child protection knowledge and skills among all staff and volunteers.

Economically and/or Socially Deprived People

StreetGames

StreetGames is an award-winning sports charity that brings sport straight to the doorstep of young people living in disadvantaged communities.

StreetGames is a network of organisations that delivers sporting opportunities to young people in England, Wales and Scotland. All projects in the StreetGames network are locally funded and controlled so group leaders know and understand the communities they work in. This is a radical but effective approach called doorstep sport.

StreetGames Training Academy

StreetGames has introduced a series of training workshops and opportunities to educate and train staff, coaches and volunteers in doorstep sport issues.

The StreetGames Training Academy will encourage:

- more people and organisations to promote doorstep sport opportunities

- local doorstep trainers delivering training to meet local community needs

- increased participation and retention rates by young people involved in sport.

StreetGames Head Office

Lilian Baylis Old School
Lollard Street
London SE11 6PY

Tel: 0845-1300 849
Email: info@streetgames.org
Website: www.streetgames.org

StreetGames Northern Office

Unit G3 Barton Hall Estate
Hardy Street
Manchester M30 7NB

Coaching Agenda

sports coach UK

Chelsea Close
Off Amberley Road
Armley
Leeds LS12 4HP

Tel: 0113-274 4802
Fax: 0113-231 9606
Email: coaching@sportscoachuk.org
Website: www.sportscoachuk.org

sports coach UK is the only organisation in the UK dedicated to the development of coaching and coaches. sports coach UK believes the composition of the coaching community should reflect that of the broader community, in terms of gender, ethnic origin and ability. However, it recognises and acknowledges that disabled people, people from minority ethnic communities, and women and girls, are under-represented in all spheres of coaching, umpiring and officiating.

sports coach UK's equity action plan outlines the way in which the organisation intends to take positive action to increase the involvement of under-represented groups within the coaching community. It is currently implementing the plan in partnership with:

- CSPs
- local authorities
- governing bodies of sport
- the five sports councils
- the four home nation disability sports organisations (EFDS, Scottish Disability Sport, Disability Sport Wales, Disability Sports Northern Ireland)
- Sporting Equals
- WSFF
- Pride Sports
- StreetGames.

sports coach UK was one of the first organisations to be awarded the Achieving Racial Equality – A Standard for Sport at preliminary level (see page 126 for further details).

For further information about sports coach UK's equity action plan, contact the Development Lead Officer for Inclusion and Diversity at the above address.

The UK Coaching Framework – A 3-7-11-Year Action Plan

The need for such a plan arises from the increasing significance to the sporting and wider government agenda of coaching in the UK. Sport has a high national profile and it is now recognised at government level throughout the UK that sport and physical activity contribute significantly to the health, social inclusion and identity of the nation. The long-term vision for sport sets out two overarching objectives to be achieved by 2020 – to increase and widen the base of participation and to achieve success on the world stage.

The UK Coaching Framework provides the blueprint for developing the system that will take coaching in the UK forwards towards the goal of being the best in the world by 2016. The Framework will ensure both the development and delivery of the coaching system is relevant across the whole of the UK, taking into account the policies, strategies and priorities of the devolved administrations and the Home Country Sports Councils.

For further information relating to this topic, please see the System, Strategy and Policy section of the sports coach UK website: www.sportscoachuk.org

Equality Agenda

The Equality and Human Rights Commission (EHRC) was launched in October 2007, taking over the role and functions of the Commission for Racial Equality, the Disability Rights Commission and the Equal Opportunities Commission, and assuming new responsibilities for sexual orientation, age, religion and belief, and human rights.

The Commission is a non-departmental public body (NDPB), established under the Equality Act 2006 as a corporate body. Its sponsor department is the Government Equalities Office, with a board of commissioners who steer the commission's work and direction.

The Commission covers Great Britain (ie England, Scotland and Wales) but not Northern Ireland. It has offices in London, Manchester, Cardiff and Glasgow, with a regional presence in nine offices in England and one in North Wales.

The EHRC focuses upon the following areas:

- enforcing the law
- influencing the development of the law and government policy
- promoting good practice
- campaigns, events and communications
- fostering better relations
- developing understanding and evidence
- its services.

Main offices

The telephone numbers of the EHRC offices below are not for the EHRC helpline. If you require this service, the helpline numbers are listed separately at the end.

London

3 More London
Riverside Tooley Street
London SE1 2RG

Tel: 020-3117 0235 (non-helpline calls only)
Fax: 020-7407 7557
Email: info@equalityhumanrights.com

Manchester

Arndale House
The Arndale Centre
Manchester M4 3AQ

Tel: 0161-829 8100 (non-helpline calls only)
Fax: 0161-829 8110
Email: info@equalityhumanrights.com

Cardiff

3rd floor
3 Callaghan Square
Cardiff CF10 5BT

Tel: 029-2044 7710 (non-helpline calls only)
Textphone: 029-2044 7713
Fax: 029-2044 7712
Email: wales@equalityhumanrights.com

Glasgow

The Optima Building
58 Robertson Street
Glasgow G2 8DU

Tel: 0141-228 5910 (non-helpline calls only)
Fax: 0141-228 5912
Email: scotland@equalityhumanrights.com

Media enquiries

If you work in the media and wish to speak to the EHRC press office, call 020-3117 0255 (out of hours mobile 07767 272 818).

Helpline

England: 0845-604 6610
Textphone: 0845-604 6620

Scotland: 0845-604 5510
Textphone: 0845-604 5520

Wales: 0845-604 8810
Textphone: 0845-604 8820

Equality Commission for Northern Ireland

Equality House
7–9 Shaftesbury Square
Belfast BT2 7DP

Tel: 028-9050 0600
Textphone: 028-9050 0589
Enquiry line: 028-9089 0890
Fax: 028-9024 8687
Email: information@equalityni.org
Website: www.equalityni.org

The Equality Commission for Northern Ireland is an independent public body established under the Northern Ireland Act 1998.

The Commission's duties and functions are set out in the legislation for which it has responsibility. General duties include:

*   working towards the elimination of discrimination

*   promoting equality of opportunity and encouraging good practice

*   promoting affirmative/positive action

*   promoting good relations between people of different racial groups

*   overseeing the implementation and effectiveness of the statutory duty on public authorities

*   keeping the relevant legislation under review.

It may not be appropriate for people to take part in sport during important religious festivals. The table below lists the main festivals celebrated by people from different religions. You should always take these into account when scheduling coaching sessions, events or competitions. The dates of the festivals may vary from year to year, so you are advised to consult the Shap Calendar of Religious Festivals[22] for details of dates in particular years.

The list is by no means exhaustive, so remember to consult with individual participants too.

Name of Festival	Religion	Description
Christmas Day	Christian	A major festival in the Christian faith, which celebrates the birth of Jesus, who Christians believe to be the Son of God. Gifts are reminders of the offerings brought to the infant Jesus.
Easter Day	Christian	The most important festival of the Christian year, when Christians celebrate the resurrection of Jesus. Easter eggs are given, which symbolise new life.
Eid ul-Fitr	Muslim	A three-day festival of the breaking of the fast, which comes at the end of Ramadan and at the start of the first of Shawwal, the 10th month of the Muslim calendar. It is a time for almsgiving, new clothes, good food, presents for children, family get-togethers and contact with friends. The community assembles for Eid prayer at the mosque or another suitable venue.
Hanamatsuri	Japanese and Buddhist	A flower festival marking the Japanese celebration of the Buddha Shakyamuni's birthday. Flowers accentuate the tradition that the Buddha was born in a garden, so floral shrines are made and an image of the infant Buddha is set in it and bathed.
Navaratri/Durga Puja/Dusserah	Hindu	One of the few festivals celebrated across India. Navaratri means nine nights, which is how long the festival lasts. The final three days are the most important.

---

[22] Available from the Shap Working Party on World Religions in Education.

Name of Festival	Religion	Description
Passover/Pesach	Jewish	A major eight-day festival when Jews commemorate the Exodus from their slavery in Egypt. A highlight is the Seder meal held in each family's home at the beginning of the festival, when the story of their deliverance is recounted. Matzah (unleavened bread) is eaten throughout the festival, as are other foods that contain no leaven.
Ramadan	Muslim	The month of fasting from dawn to sunset. To Muslims, fasting means abstaining from all food, drink, smoking and marital relations during daylight hours. It is an exercise in self-discipline and enables everyone to have some experience of deprivation. The fast is traditionally broken each evening by taking dates and water. Children may be encouraged to fast, although the full fast is not compulsory until maturity.
Yom Kippur	Jewish	The final day of the 10 days of repentance. It is the holiest day of the year in the Jewish calendar. The Bible calls it the Sabbath of Sabbaths and it is marked by afflicting the soul – expressed through a total fast lasting 25 hours. Jews spend most of the eve and most of the day in prayer.

New Year Festivals

Some of the New Year festivals celebrated by people from different religions are listed below:

- Al-Hijra (Muslim)

- Chaitra (Hindu)

- Divali/Deepavali (Hindu)

- Ethiopian New Year's Day (Rastafarian)

- Ganjitsu (Japanese)

- Rosh Hashana (Jewish)

- Vaisakhi (Baisakhi) (Sikh)

- Yuan Tan (Chinese).

This list is not exhaustive, so remember to consult with individual participants too.

The text in this appendix is based on information from the *Shap Calendar of Religious Festivals*. Reproduced with the kind permission of the Shap Working Party on World Religions in Education.

Most people want to treat disabled employees, job applicants and customers the same way as everyone else, but aren't always sure how to go about it. These suggestions aren't part of the DDA 1995 and 2004, but they may be useful when you meet disabled people.

Remember!

- Disabled people are individuals just like everybody else. Don't make assumptions about their abilities or their needs. Don't forget that some impairments are hidden (eg epilepsy and mental illness).

- If you aren't sure how something might affect a disabled person, ask that person for advice.

- Coaching disabled people allows you to develop your existing ability to **differentiate**. But do not assume that just because someone has an impairment they are any less able than any of your other participants.

Communication

- If a disabled person is accompanied by a non-disabled friend, relative or support worker, talk to the disabled person directly. This also applies to a deaf person accompanied by a sign language interpreter.

- When talking to a deaf person, find out whether he lip-reads. If he does:

  - make sure your face is in the light/you are not standing with the light directly behind you

  - look directly at the person

  - speak clearly and naturally – don't overempasise your words

  - remember to keep your hands away from your face.

- When you first meet a visually impaired person, introduce yourself. When you are going to move away, tell her. Don't leave her talking to an empty space.

- When you are talking to someone with a speech impairment, concentrate on what is being said, be patient and don't try to guess what she wants to say. If you don't understand, don't pretend you do.

- If someone has difficulty understanding you (perhaps because they have a learning disability), be patient and be prepared to explain something more than once. Concentrate on using simple language.

- When talking to a wheelchair user, try to ensure your eyes are at the same level as his, perhaps by sitting down. Don't lean on the wheelchair – it is part of the user's personal space.

- Avoid asking personal questions about a person's impairment, such as: 'were you born like that?' An employer could ask: 'does your disability affect your ability to do this job?'

- If someone looks different, avoid staring. Concentrate on what she is saying, not on the way she looks.

- If you are talking to an adult, treat him like an adult.

Assistance

- If someone looks as if she needs assistance, offer it, but wait for her to accept before you help.

- When guiding a visually impaired person, do not push or pull him. Ask if he would like to take hold of your arm. If there are any steps, tell him whether the steps go up or down. Give a description of the environment using the 'clock' method (eg 'lift at 10 o'clock, bookcase at one o'clock').

- Remember that guide dogs for visually impaired people, hearing dogs for deaf people and other assistance dogs are working dogs, not pets. They should not be fed, patted or distracted when they are working.

- Above all, treat everyone as you would expect to be treated yourself.

The text above is based on information from DL200 (guidelines issued on behalf of the Minister for Disabled People. Prepared in conjunction with the National Disability Council and RADAR). Reproduced with the kind permission of RADAR.

Language

Some of the words and phrases we use offend disabled people, because they suggest that the disabled person is dependent or helpless. Some words, such as 'cripple' or 'retarded', have become terms of abuse or are used to make fun of disabled people. Below are some common words to avoid, with suggested alternatives:

- Do not say 'the disabled', use 'disabled people'.

- Do not say 'suffering from', 'crippled by', 'afflicted by' or 'a victim of', use 'a person who has' or 'a person with'.

- Do not say 'deaf and dumb', use 'deaf without speech'.

- Do not say 'an epileptic', use 'a person with epilepsy'.

- Do not say 'spastic', use 'a person with cerebral palsy'.

- Do not say 'mentally handicapped' or 'subnormal', use 'a person with a learning disability'.

- Do not say 'confined to a wheelchair' or 'wheelchair bound', use 'wheelchair user'.

Coaching People with Learning Disabilities

- Be patient, tolerant, consistent and tactful, but ensure that participants understand the boundaries of acceptable behaviour.

- Break down complex skills into smaller steps.

- Establish the level to which instructions and directions are understood.

- Avoid using abstract models or diagrams.

- Facilitate simple decision making.

- Avoid drills that rely heavily on numeracy and literacy skills.

- Coach by showing and copying, not telling.

- Be aware that the motor skills and physical fitness of some participants may be generally poor due to lack of opportunities to participate in sporting activities, or even take regular day-to-day exercise.

African	A native inhabitant of the continent of Africa. A person of African descent or ancestry. Africans are generally divided into North Africans (north of the Sahara desert) and Sub-Saharan Africans (south of the Sahara desert).
Asian	A native inhabitant of the continent of Asia. A person of Asian descent or ancestry. Asians are generally divided into South Asians, who are mainly of Indian origin, and Orientals, who are mainly of Chinese and Japanese origin.
Black-British/ British-born Black	In its narrowest sense, this term refers to British-born British citizens of African or Caribbean descent.
British-born African	A person of African descent or ancestry born in Great Britain.
British-born Asian	A person of Asian descent or ancestry born in Great Britain.
British-born Caribbean	A person of Caribbean descent or ancestry born in Great Britain.
Caribbean	A native inhabitant of the Caribbean.
Country of birth	The actual country where an individual was born. Country of birth is distinct from nationality or ethnicity.
Country of origin	The birthplace of a person and/or parents and, in some instances, grandparents.
Culture	The customary beliefs, social forms and material traits of racial, ethnic, religious or social groups. Socially patterned human thought and behaviour. Culture is social heritage or tradition that is passed on to future generations. It is shared, learnt human behaviour – a way of life.
Customs	Habitual course of action, usual behaviour and a particular, established way of behaving.
Ethnic	Relates to large groups of people classed according to common nationality, traits, customs, culture and traditions. Ethnicity is more likely to denote origin or birth than political nationality.
Ethnic origin	One's parentage and ancestry (racial and geographical).
Minority ethnic	An ethnic group within a society or region that is smaller in numbers than the majority population. A minority population is often a group of people whose group members have significantly less control or power over their lives than members of a majority group.
Mixed race/biracial/ dual heritage	The offspring of a union between persons of different races.
Multicultural	Reflecting more than one cultural group; diverse cultures.

Plural society	A form of society embracing many majority groups and cultural traditions.
Race relations	Inter-racial/ethnic connections, usually for the promotion and maintenance of mutual interest, involvement and benefits of all the groups concerned.
Racial	Concerning groups of individuals identifiable or differentiated by race.
Racialism	Discriminatory actions resulting from racist beliefs.
Racism	Conduct, words or practices that advantage or disadvantage people because of their colour, culture or ethnic origin.
Racist	One who believes that populations should be categorised based on physical genetic features, that some races or ethnic groups are superior to others, and that inferior groups should not have the same basic human rights as their superiors.
South Asian	A native inhabitant or descendant of southern Asia, including India, Pakistan, Bangladesh and Sri Lanka.
Tradition	An inherited, established or customary pattern of thought or action. Beliefs and customs handed down, generally by word of mouth, or by behaviour.
West Indian	A native inhabitant of one of the Caribbean islands, which were formerly British colonies, known as the West Indian islands, together with British Guyana and British Honduras. The majority population of the (former) West Indian islands is made up of peoples of African, South Indian and Oriental ancestry. Caucasian (white) persons are prevalent in most of the islands.
White-English	The indigenous population of England (and Wales).
White-other	The minority white population in England, usually not English born, or second-generation whites.

Definitions adapted from *Clean Bowl Racism: A Report on Racial Equality in Cricket*. Reproduced with the kind permission of the ECB Racism Study Group.

The Inclusion Spectrum provides five ways for you to change your approach to planning a coaching session to include disabled people.

Modified activity

In a modified activity, everyone does the same task but with changes to rules, areas or equipment (eg in tennis, allowing people with mobility difficulties an extra bounce before having to return the ball).

Parallel activity

In a parallel activity, everyone participates in the same type of activity, but different groups participate in different ways and at different levels. Participants can be grouped according to skill, fitness or the way they play the game (eg a group of participants can be split into three smaller groups for a ball passing game such as netball). The rules, equipment and playing area can be different in all three groups to suit the requirements of the group that is playing.

Open activity

In an open activity, everyone does the same thing, without adaptation or modification, regardless of impairment (eg deaf athletes doing exactly the same training schedule as hearing athletes during a track or field session).

Separate activity

In a separate activity, disabled participants play separately, either as individuals or in teams (eg when a group of disabled players practise together as a team preparing for a volleyball or tennis competition that has adapted rules to suit the needs and abilities of the individuals playing).

Disability sport activity

In a disability sport activity, a group of non-disabled participants take part in an activity that has a disability sport focus. This is reverse integration (eg non-disabled players playing a game of basketball that has been adapted and modified to meet the needs and abilities of the disabled players in the group).

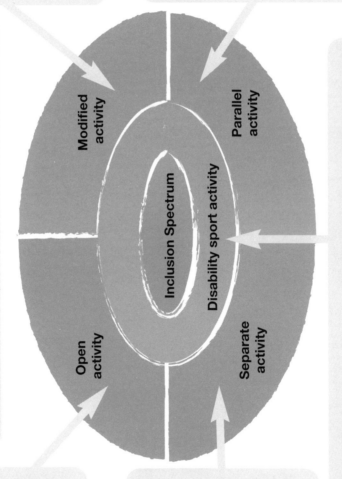

The Inclusion Spectrum

© Stevenson and Black (adapted from Stevenson, 2007[23])

[23] Stevenson, P. (2007) *Including Young Disabled People and SEN Pupils in FUNdamentals and Multi-skill Opportunities*. Loughborough: Youth Sport Trust (unpublished draft document).

This appendix contains a blank copy of the action plans used in Activity 11 (pages 99–101) for you to photocopy and use as and when required

SHORT-TERM IMPROVEMENTS/CHANGES		
What?	How?	When?
1		
2		
3		

LONG-TERM IMPROVEMENTS/CHANGES		
What?	How?	When?
1		
2		
3		

Our Vision
What we would like to see

UK coaching excellence enabling all children, players and athletes to follow their dreams, have fun and fulfil their potential.

Our Mission
Why we exist

To support our UK partners to recruit, develop and retain coaches to achieve their participation and performance goals (in the context of The UK Coaching Framework).

Our Strategic Objectives
What we will do

To achieve our mission, we will:

1   champion and drive policy and investment in coaching

2   support and challenge our partners to improve their coaching systems and grow their contribution to a cohesive UK coaching system

3   provide products and services that add value to our partners' coaching systems and their coaches

4   provide research and share good practice that will benefit coaching

5   develop quality leadership, good governance and a skilled team to ensure an effective UK coaching agency.